Song of the Open Road

Song of the Open Road, 1

Afoot and light-hearted I take to the open road,
Healthy, free, the world before me,
The long brown path before me leading wherever I choose.
Henceforth I ask not good-fortune, I myself am good-fortune,
Henceforth I whimper no more, postpone no more, need nothing,
Done with indoor complaints, libraries, querulous criticisms,
Strong and content I travel the open road.
The earth, that is sufficient,
I do not want the constellations any nearer,
I know they are very well where they are,
I know they suffice for those who belong to them.
(Still here I carry my old delicious burdens,
I carry them, men and women, I carry them with me wherever I go,
I swear it is impossible for me to get rid of them,
I am fill'd with them, and I will fill them in return.) ...

Walt Whitman, 1855

38TH STUDENT POETRY CONTEST HONOREES
5.5.2024

Featuring WWBA 2024 Poet in Residence

Linda Gregerson

Copyright © 2024 Walt Whitman Birthplace
All rights reserved.

Published by Red Penguin Books

ISBN
Digital 978-1-63777-584-4
Print 978-1-63777-585-1

No part of this book may be reproduced in any form or by any electronic or mechanical means, including information storage and retrieval systems, without written permission from the author, except for the use of brief quotations in a book review.

All individual works are copyrighted to the writers.

Dear Readers,

Walt Whitman Birthplace Association (WWBA) congratulates the student poets in this anthology for their writing excellence! Each student embraced Whitman's optimistic ode to wanderlust as illustrated in his famous work, Song of the Open Road, and created a unique response shaped in the spirit of Walt's free verse poetry. We invite you to step into their world through the vision, words, and images of the talented honorees of our 38th Annual Student Poetry Writing Contest.

In 2024, we received more than 2000 entries from across the world, and a panel of published poets served as judges. We thank judges Linda Dickman, Nancy Keating and Cheryl Williams for their time and professional collaboration. We acknowledge the students in this publication for their outstanding achievement, and we applaud their parents and teachers, who guide and support their educational and creative endeavors.

Many new poets embrace poetic license. The editors have aimed to remain true to the young poets' experimental use of free verse form as the students bravely struggle to embrace their multitudes. This collection celebrates their poetic voices and personal discoveries.

Linda Gregerson, the WWBA 2024 Poet in Residence, Deciduous, joined the celebration awards and offered words of praise and encouragement to the student poets. She read her poem and contributed its printing and sale as a Limited-edition Broadside of 100 copies to support our education programs.

We deeply value our local, national, and international support which helps us to fulfill our mission to preserve and promote the legacy of Walt Whitman at this NY State Historic Site where he was born in 1819. Throughout the year, we host poetry readings and workshops, art exhibits, literary activities, community programs and seasonal family events.

As a non-profit organization, the success of our programs is directly linked to the generosity of individuals like you who understand the importance of the unique role we serve. Please support our mission in any way that appeals to you – join, donate, sponsor, visit, volunteer, promote!

Let us now celebrate the young poets in this Anthology. We look forward to their continued literary accomplishments in the spirit of Walt Whitman.

Sincerely,

Walt Whitman Birthplace Association

Linda Gregerson

The WWBA's 2024 Poet in Residence Linda Gregerson is the author of seven books of poetry, most recently of Canopy (Ecco/HarperCollins 2022). Her second collection (The Woman Who Died in Her Sleep, Houghton Mifflin 1996) was a finalist for the Lenore Marshall Prize; her third (Waterborne, Houghton Mifflin 2002) won the Kingsley Tufts Poetry Prize; her fourth (Magnetic North, Houghton Mifflin 2007) was a finalist for the National Book Award. She has also published two critical monographs and numerous essays on early modern English and contemporary American poetry.

Linda's poems have appeared in The New Yorker, The Atlantic, London Review of Books, Poetry Review, and a host of other literary journals. Among her honors are awards from the American Academy of Arts and Letters and the Poetry Society of America and fellowships from the National Endowment for the Arts, the National Humanities Center, the Guggenheim, Rockefeller, and Mellon Foundations, and the Institute for Advanced Study.

A fellow of the American Academy of Arts and Sciences and former Chancellor of the Academy of American Poets, Linda is the Caroline Walker Bynum Distinguished University Professor at the University of Michigan, where she directs the Helen Zell Writers' Program. She divides her time between Ann Arbor, Michigan, and London.

DECIDUOUS
Linda Gregerson

Speak plainly, said November to the maples, say
    what you mean now, now

that summer's lush declensions lie like the lies
    they were at your feet. Haven't

we praised you? Haven't we summer after summer
    put our faith in augmentation.

But look at these leavings of not-enough-light:
    it's time for sterner counsel now.

It's time, we know you're good at this, we've
    seen the way your branched

articulations keep faith with the whole, it's time
    to call us back to order before

we altogether lose our way.   Speak
    brightly, said the cold months, speak

with a mouth of snow. The scaffolding is
    clear now, we thank you, the moon

can measure its course by you. Instruct us,
    while the divisions of light

are starkest, before the murmurs of con-
    solation resume, instruct us in

the harder course of mindfulness.
    Speak   truly, said April. Not just

what you think we're hoping to hear, speak
    so we believe you.

The child who learned perspective from the
    stand of you, near and nearer,

knowing you were permanent, is counting
    the years to extinction now. Teach her

to teach us the disciplines of do-less-harm. We're
    capable of learning. We've glimpsed

the bright intelligence that courses through the body
    that contains us.   *De +*

cidere, say the maples, has another face.
    It also means decide.

    Reprinted from Linda Gregerson, Canopy. New York:
    Mariner/HarperCollins, 2022.

Acknowledgments

We would like to thank our new Executive Director Caitlyn Shea and the Board of Trustees who offer their outstanding guidance and support for all Association endeavors. Together, they extend the following acknowledgements on behalf of Walt Whitman Birthplace Association (WWBA):

We thank all the student poets in this anthology who sustain the spirit of Walt Whitman with their creative and diverse voices. We thank all parents, teachers and mentors who foster poetry by teaching the value of words.

WWBA offers gratitude to our annual Poets in Residence, specifically Linda Gregerson this year, who serve to illuminate and fulfill the legacy of Walt Whitman with their teachings and own writing. We thank the contest judges, Nancy Keating, Linda Dickman and Sheryl Williams, poets themselves who read every poem and delight in celebrating the creative verses of the students. We thank the professional staff who make all our educational programs happen so effortlessly.

Our programs are facilitated by Curator Margaret Guardi, Event & Media Director Heather Famiglietti, Education Director Lisa Pulitzer, Administrator Derry Shafer, Controller Bonnie Meder, Poetry Educators Linda Trott Dickman, Laurie Rozakis, PhD, and Jack Canfora, Art Educator Lena Sawyer, Docents Jim Broten, Jack Canfora, Jonathan Kalish, Danny Korez, Barbara Nelson, Cameron Williams and Donna Varon, long term volunteers Bruce Johnson, Lauren Montgomery, Nancy Newkirk, Alice Wilson and Mechale Clyde, Caretaker John Murray, and a multitude of dedicated interns. A special thanks to our loyal Whitman Personator Darrel Blaine Ford, who makes sure Whitman shows up every year for all the students.

WWBA offers appreciation to New York State Office of Parks, Recreation and Historic Preservation with individual recognition going to Governor Kathy Hochul, Parks Commissioner Eric Kulleseid, and Long Island Regional Director George Gorman. We greatly thank Suffolk County for their outstanding and generous support, and we acknowledge The Town of Huntington who nurtured Walt during his formative years and who continues to nurture his legacy today. We extend our appreciation to grantors The Claire Friedlander Family Foundation, Humanities New York, NYS Council on the Arts, Huntington Arts Council, and Poets & Writers for their support of literature, literacy, and learners.

We acknowledge with great appreciation our members, donors and sponsors whose contributions sustain the daily operations of the Walt Whitman Birthplace State Historic Site, and whose actions sustain the spirit of Walt Whitman.

We especially thank Publisher Stephanie Larkin of Red Penguin Books for bringing this book to fruition.

Contents

CATEGORY A — INDIVIDUAL POEM, GRADES 3 & 4

My Life's Winding Road — 2
Calissa Wong E.M. Baker Elementary School
GRAND CHAMPION 1st PLACE

Wanderlust — 3
Thomas Yeamans, Mount Sinai Elementary School
GRAND CHAMPION 2nd PLACE

Field of Flowers — 4
Deepika Joshi, Burns Avenue School
GRAND CHAMPION 3rd PLACE

My Path — 5
Annabelle Silecchia, Connolly Elementary School

The Open Road — 6
Christopher Rahner, Birchwood Intermediate School

Outstretching Land — 7
Desi Schmuhl, Saint Ann's School

Song of a Rocky Mountain — 8
Gabriel Marano, Trinity Regional School

The Soccer Champ — 9
John Bailey, The Laurel Hill School

Gaia's Land — 10
Addison Bernstein, Mount Sinai Elementary School

The Road of Life — 11
Maggie Rubin, North Side Elementary School

CATEGORY B   INDIVIDUAL POEM, GRADES 5 & 6

Pictures **Annabel Xu**, Barron Park Elementary, Palo Alto, CA GRAND CHAMPION 1st PLACE	14
The Southern Road **Nolan Berry**, Tuckahoe Common Middle School GRAND CHAMPION 2nd PLACE	15
Life's Surprises **Daniel Garcia**, The Laurel Hill School GRAND CHAMPION 3rd PLACE	16
The Open Road of No Stress **Brendan Doyle**, Tuckahoe Common Middle School	17
Where I Want to Go **Cathleen Annello**, St. Dominic Elementary	18
Golden Hour **Emily Gravitz**, Lakeville Elementary School	19
The Joys of Travel **Grace-Marie Jones**, Holy Child Academy	20
No Other Way for Me **Noora Ahmed**, Bay Shore Middle School	21
The Foggy Road **Janae Henry**, The Laurel Hill School	22
Towards the Ever Blazing Sun **Oorja Anand Singh**, Roslyn Middle School	23
On the Old Valley **Parnav Chadha**, Burns Avenue School	24
Farther **Weizheng Evalyn Chen**, West Lafayette Intermediate School, Indiana	25

CATEGORY C INDIVIDUAL POEM, GRADES 7 & 8

In Hopes of Finding Myself Once More 28
Shreya Satpathy, W.T. Clarke Middle School
GRAND CHAMPION 1ST PLACE

They Call Her Liberty 29
Ziya Yin, P.J. Galinas Junior High School
GRAND CHAMPION 2ND PLACE

A One-Way Journey 30
Stephanie Green, Bay Shore Middle School
GRAND CHAMPION 3RD PLACE

Storm 31
Alexa Surdi, Mount Sinai Middle School

Dense Air 32
Ariel Ruggiero, Springs School

Colors of the Open Road 33
Evelyn Sanders, Friends Academy

Belly of the Beast 34
Gianna Fitzpatrick, Wantagh Middle School

My Forged Path 35
Janis Fok, Great Neck South Middle School

The Journey of Life 36
Nicole Kolasny, St. Aiden School

Untitled 37
Nora Aziz, New Hyde Park Memorial High School

North Wind 38
Patrick Baynon, Holy Child Academy

Through a path with... 39
Pinar Isildak, P.J. Gelinas Junior High School

The Closed Road — 40
Sara Martella, St. Dominic Elementary and Middle School

Shards — 41
Yuri Montas, Floral Park Memorial High School

CATEGORY D INDIVIDUAL POEM, GRADES 9 & 10

Grass — 44
Jacob Torczyner, David Renov Stahler Yeshiva High School for Boys
GRAND CHAMPION 1ST PLACE

The Winding Path — 45
Allen Sinai, Manhasset Secondary School
GRAND CHAMPION 2ND PLACE

Arboraceous Wanderer — 46
William Pereira, Manhasset Secondary School
GRAND CHAMPION 3RD PLACE

Unbound — 47
Alexis Thomas, Manhasset Secondary School

My Road Is Me — 48
AnaLuz Ferrer, Oyster Bay High School

Hello — 49
Giuliana DePaola, Floral Park Memorial High School

Story of My Life — 50
Grace Kuskowski, New Hyde Park Memorial High School

The Ballad of Footsteps — 51
Isabella Fernandim, Sacred Heart Academy

Echoes of Abandoned Dreams — 52
Madison Bruck, Manhasset Secondary School

Journey of the Open Road — 53
Matilda Saltiel, POB JFK High School

The Road of Life   54
Sebastian Song, New Hyde Park Memorial High School

Nature's Road   55
Thomas Matranga, Chaminade High School

Retrace   56
Veronica Qiu, Palo Alto High School, Palo Alto, CA

CATEGORY E   INDIVIDUAL POEM, GRADES 11 & 12

4:00 AM Tuesdays at the Airport   58
Jiwan Kim, Horace Mann School, Bronx, NY
GRAND CHAMPION 1ST PLACE

anatomy of a hodophile   59
Rina Olsen, St. John's School, Guam
GRAND CHAMPION 2ND PLACE

Onions   60
Damaris Sumba Lliguin, Bellport High School
GRAND CHAMPION 3RD PLACE

i am free jazz   61
Andrew Fogel, Walt Whitman High School

to walk the poet road   62
Sarah Sun, Great Neck South High School

A woman's "open road"   63
Alissa Olivera, North Babylon High School

Keys or Gate   64
Aurelia Turano, Walt Whitman High School

Road Trip to 2014   65
Benjamin Wang, Dougherty Valley High School,
San Ramon, CA

loose change **Elaina Li**, Roslyn High School	66
Buddhism in the Morning **Evan Wang**, Upper Merion High School, King of Prussia, PA	67
9 and a half **Jeffrey Valle**, Walt Whitman High School	68
th(ink) **John Zsamboky**, Chaminade High School	69
Domesticated Poetry **Nuala Mernin**, Saint Ann's School	70
Destiny; Manifested **Olivia Robitsek**, Ward Melville High School	71

CATEGORY G   CLASS ANTHOLOGY, GRADES 3 & 4

Birch Pages Writing Club **Ms. Lopez**, Birch School, Grades 3 & 4 GRAND CHAMPION	74

CATEGORY I   CLASS ANTHOLOGY, GRADES 7 & 8

Our Journeys **Nicole Pomaro**, Mount Sinai Middle School, Grade 8, Period 9 GRAND CHAMPION	82

Sailing Spartans: A Collection of Off-Beat Journeys   106
Karl O'Leary, Sodus Central School District,
Grade 8, Period 6

Where the Road Ends   106
Kelly Doran, Mount Sinai Middle School,
Grade 7, Period 3

The Door to Dreams   107
Kelly Doran, Mount Sinai Middle School,
Grade 7, Period 7

Away We Go   107
Nicole Pomaro, Mount Sinai Middle School,
Grade 8, Period 4

Encounters on Life's Road   107
Nicole Wallace, Mount Sinai Middle School,
Grade 8, Period 6

CATEGORY J   CLASS ANTHOLOGY, GRADES 9 & 10

Alliance poétique!   110
Clare Chotiner, Hicksville High School,
Grade 9, Period 3
GRAND CHAMPION

Vastness   160
Melissa Martin, Eastport-South Manor Jr/Sr High School,
Period 1

Paths Unpaved   160
Shannon Murphy, Oyster Bay High School,
Grade 9, Period 3

Avenues Await   160
Shannon Murphy, Oyster Bay High School,
Grade 9, Period 6

CATEGORY K — CLASS ANTHOLOGY, GRADES 11 & 12

The Road of Desire — 162
Deirdre Faughey, Oyster Bay High School,
Grade 11, Period 2
GRAND CHAMPION

The Next Road — 172
Deirdre Faughey, Oyster Bay High School,
Grade 11, Period 4

Road Conditions — 172
Maria Kim, Oyster Bay High School,
Grade 11, Period 1

Sunshowers — 172
Maria Kim, Oyster Bay High School,
Grade 11, Period 8

CATEGORY L — MULTIMEDIA

A Journey into the Unknown — 176
Madison Kelly, Mount Sinai Middle School
GRAND CHAMPION

INDIVIDUAL POEM, GRADES 3 & 4

Category A

Grand Champion 1st Place

My Life's Winding Road
Calissa Wong

An adventurer I am, I take on life's winding road.
I know that hills and mountains are before me, rough patches that I may have to climb
Though that might be tough, people around me are there to help me through thick and thin.
They are just like the bright shining sun and the rain water,
helping the plants surrounding me grow continuously through different weather and storms.

Walking along the open road, in the morning, I can smell the freshness of the air.
The crisp morning air makes me feel renewed and refreshed,
Just like doing morning exercises with my classmates at school.
Sometimes though, the air smells different... damp, dry or smoky.
During those times, I need the comfort of friends to get through the day.

At times, life's journey takes me to paths in hidden forests.
Hearing the birds chirping makes me feel warm, like my mother's hug around me.
At night, the forest's paths are dark and misty,
Surprisingly, lightning bugs and stars come out to bring light to the path,
Just like guidance by my teachers and coaches.

I am able to walk through life's various roads,
I know that what I learn along my path and the various people I meet, will guide me through.
I am thankful that people are there to support me every step of the way.
In the same way, I know that I will guide the paths of others that I meet along the way
Using the past experiences that I have along my journey; I will fill their bucket like they filled mine.

Category A, Individual Poem Grades 3–4
E.M. BAKER ELEMENTARY SCHOOL
Mrs. Cori Pahl

Grand Champion 2nd Place

Wanderlust
Thomas Yeamans

I shall frolic on a long expedition. The path is miles long,
And no one has reached the end. With my enormous sack of essentials, I seek the fascinating thing of life.
What fronts me is the first obstacle.
A tree that's the size of the Burj Khalifa!
So, I take a bold leap of faith,
And jump over the monstrous trunk.
Continuing on my meander I discover a milestone.
It reads, "Mile 1/25." But I venture on, Despite my fatigue,
Wanderlust keeps me going. I venture on.
Later a bunny runs with a rainstorm.
From the mountains it grows like mushrooms. So, I take to a hut.
I need to move,
So, I take again on my journey.

Category A, Individual Poem Grades 3–4

MOUNT SINAI ELEMENTARY SCHOOL
Mr. Kevin Walsh

Grand Champion 3rd Place

Field of Flowers
Deepika Joshi

I don't know where I'm going.
It could be anywhere, anywhere.
I guess I'll just have to explore this new world and make some choices.
I'm far from my home, here there will be many opportunities and challenges.
Running and running, I feel so alive than I've ever been! My feet pounding on the cold, hard surface of the road.
My heart is beating so loudly, it sounds like thunder and lightning! It's raining now.
Sometimes I feel like I should choose to go back to my comfy house filled with my friends and family.
But I choose to continue and explore this new world. I'm in a field of flowers now.
There's a little pink butterfly flying just above a flower.
The butterfly now starts to gracefully fly into the forest, like it's trying to tell me something.
Should I follow the butterfly?
Maybe it's trying to tell me something! Maybe it's giving me a new path to follow! I guess I'll see!
I start to run, hearing my heartbeat quicken as I follow the little pink butterfly.
I turn left.
Then I turn right.
It just stopped raining.
The leaves are wet. Should I drink the raindrops? Yeah, yeah I should.
I see a portal, should I step in? I'll step in...

Category A, Individual Poem Grades 3–4
BURNS AVENUE SCHOOL
Ms. Alison Urkiel

 ## Honorable Mentions

My Path
Annabelle Silecchia

On my road, my long, long path, I walk, not knowing what is ahead, But knowing that I am safe on it, wild and free,

Smelling flowers and air along the way.

On my road, my wonderful path, there are rocks and trees in my way, I fight through.

Birds chirp highly, high into the trees, on their own path, I wonder what their path is like.

But I am on my own.

As my journey goes on, pebbles and branches get stuck in my shoe.

I stop, take them out and keep going.

I get cuts and bruises, but I keep going.

I keep going, and walking.

Sometimes I feel like running,

And sometimes like stopping, But I keep going.

Sometimes the path is beautiful like a daisy, but sometimes It is ugly like a swamp.

Sometimes the path is sweet, and sometimes it is sour.

Sometimes I trip and fall, But I have to get back up.

My path is My path, And I keep walking.

And at the end of the path, I will only get to a new one, for my life has only begun, and yours has too.

Category A, Individual Poem Grades 3–4
CONNOLLY ELEMENTARY SCHOOL
Mr. Bryce Klatsky

The Open Road
Christopher Rahner

I went out of my house one day and saw the open road.
I begged to go down that road, that road everyone knows. And so that day I strolled down that wide road
That open road that goes and goes.
I looked around the busy road while I strolled on the sidewalk I heard lots of kids talking and drawing with chalk
The road wound around the water while birds swirled in the air I smelled nice roses along a fence there
I went onto the road and I wasn't afraid
I watched in a tree where a little bird laid Some baby birds were still in their eggs
I looked up at them and then down at my legs I set off again, ready to explore
I knew this very road had a bit more
I touched a green bush on the side of the road That road, that road that everyone knows Enjoying nature and all the rest
The open road's adventures are the best

Category A, Individual Poem Grades 3–4
BIRCHWOOD INTERMEDIATE SCHOOL
Mr Stephen Corbellini

Outstretching Land
Desi Schmuhl

The land stretches out
New smells and tastes on the way
With thoughts anew waiting
I walk on

Branches twisted twirling
Daisies in the breeze
They feel of fuzz and smell of peace
I still stride on

Growing buds
Someone speaking
Grass tingles the tips of my toes
Yet I still glide on

Never reaching the end

  But something like this
      Do ends even exist?

Song of a Rocky Mountain
Gabriel Marano

Happily I hike over the mountain before me.
Happily and free, the world before me.
The rocky path before me.
Henceforth I have no fortune.
I myself am good.
I am the fortune.
When it is night, I camp on the mountain before me.
When the morning wakes, it wakes me.
I go up the mountain.
I go to set the camp before me.
 The night creeps, but I fight.
The mean creeps of night. And
then I go off the mountain.
Off, off and away I go down the mountain.
When I make it down, I am going off and off.
To my house I go to rest after a hard day of work.

Category A, Individual Poem Grades 3–4
TRINITY REGIONAL SCHOOL
Mrs. Cindy Rahner

The Soccer Champ
John Bailey

My life road is going to be an amazing soccer player.
I will travel the miles for every game.
I will run, run,run as fast as I can up and down the field in the hot sun.
I become tired, my legs feel like ice cream on a summer day.
I need to stop, rest and relax
But nothing can stop me from playing.
When the time is right, I can kick POW! BONG! BOOM!
The ball goes soaring like a bird that has mastered flight.
Into the net it goes
Then, cheering comes like the roar of a lion.
Tomorrow I could have another opponent stronger, faster and better than me.
I try and try to be better, but I can't .
I start thinking down on myself, my own skill, and I quit.
I still practice on my own, in my space and I slowly become more confident
And better than myself before.
I break my records and my achievements
Not anyone else's records.
Then I give the team one more try and continue to better myself.
I run, run, run up and down the field toward the goal and KICK!
The ball flies through the air and into the open net.
On my huge journey I have learned to not to be better than my opponent,
But myself first!

Gaia's Land
Addison Bernstein

Adventure awaits on the journey I take.
It feels like a wave of wanderlust washed over me.
I hear nature calling to me,
My journey begins.
The whispering wind blows,
The trees, like swings, sway side to
side. I see the river running and
leaping.
I think about everything I've left behind.
But the journey I'm taking makes me
happy. I hear something in the distance,
What could it be?

Category A, Individual Poem Grades 3–4
MT. SINAI ELEMENTARY SCHOOL
Mr. Kevin Walsh

The Road of Life
Maggie B. Rubin

Two roads diverged,
On a cold winter–

One with dark and fear:
Where trees leaned in on me,
The mountains closed in around me,
Making me feel trapped,
in gray grass–

The other with light and celebration:
Where the sun shone down–
On the dark green trees,
And the bright green grass,
With nice mellow hills–

I stood motionless
Not knowing what to do.

They merged together,
And I kept moving forward,
And followed the path of life–
Through both light and dark–
Through both sad and happy–
Through all the contradictions,
Through all of life's multitudes.

I will keep moving forward.

Category A, Individual Poem Grades 3–4
NORTH SIDE ELEMENTARY SCHOOL
Mrs. Stefanie Granville

INDIVIDUAL POEM, GRADES 5 & 6

Category B

Grand Champion 1st Place

Pictures
Annabel Xu

We will bring our suitcases, full of cotton shirts and cotton sweatpants
that never make us sweat. I'll sit in the back seat with my brother, side by side,
the bags of trail mix and crackers between us—they'll be empty soon.
In nature, we'll see the redwoods, blushing monkey flowers,
fruit stands selling strawberries by fields of green, and a valley
where a herd of cows lounge, snacking on grass like I snack on crackers.
The styles of music will change—from pop, to country, to jazz.
The GPS will guess, turn left, turn right, straight ahead!
Stinky ponds will season the air and gravel will make the car jump.
We'll look for diners to fill ourselves with chicken and waffles.
We'll drink some sweet hot chocolate, finally full, from chatting and chewing.
Once we come out of that place, the outside world will make us shiver
but we'll be in the car again and the heaters will make us sweat.
A red Honda, with another family mouthing words, will pass us.
They'll point at the fields and laugh, as if they told a funny joke.
The sky will be bright; I might close my eyes,
with the cold window on my forehead.
The frost on the glass won't freeze my skin
because I am covered in safe wraps.
The next thing will be a call from Mom, *We're here.*
I will stretch my legs. There will be pins and needles in my toes.
The icy ground might make me slip.
The sounds of my swishy turquoise jacket
will blend with the wind we barely hear.
The tips of big white mountains might float in the sky,
the bottoms unseen. Little spikes on snowflakes
will melt in our hands. The new fragrance of our hotel room
will take a little getting used to, but my brother and I will race
to dibs our beds. We'll take pictures to print out later;
the frames will be their forever home.

Category B, Individual Poem Grades 5–6
BARRON PARK ELEMENTARY
Shromila Gupta

# Grand Champion 2nd Place

The Southern Road
Nolan Berry

I am leaving the cold behind

The quiet birds, The bare trees, and The icy air.
My heartbeat speeds up as the excitement builds.
As I head for the road at the golden hour.
The morning dew glistens on the leaves.
The warm breeze reminds me of my grandparents' house.
I can almost smell the red velvet cake from their kitchen
I carry memories of friends and family and things I love.
Passing by the old farm at sunset, the planets and stars are appearing in the sky
I see lazy lizards lying on the side of the road.
The air is getting warmer.

I am almost at my destination at the end of the southern road.

Category B, Individual Poem Grades 5–6
TUCKAHOE COMMON MIDDLE SCHOOL
Alison Goldberg

Grand Champion 3rd Place

Life's Surprises
Daniel Garcia

With peering eyes, I stare to the heavens covered with brown arms and green hands reaching for the clouds
Standing there, not sure where I am nor uncertain of my next move
Lonely paths and empty trails surround me
Endless possibilities, opportunities await and choices to make
Silence and stillness pulsate in my mind
Moisture in the air, pine scents overwhelm my sense of smell
Vibrant blues, reds, greens, yellows, and oranges are calling,
Dark, gloomy, and mysterious paths intrigue me.

Inching towards the glaring bright lights,
Faint voices call out from the fog.
Wanting to venture into the unknown,
I go off into the mist.
Damp and cold, I trek uphill and almost slip off a cliff.
I pull myself together, and resist turning back.
In solitude with my thoughts,
Fighting with myself, I move forward.
Intentionally putting one foot in front of another,

I see people turning around and others stopping in their tracks.
After a long journey, my feet throbbing from blisters,
Famished and parched, a blurry image appears in the far distance.
Approaching, I come to a life-sized mirror.
Taking a step through, it presents me toward the brighter paths or surrendering,
Full of regrets, full of despair and becoming the bare minimum.
I backtrack to reality, where the voices get louder.

The presence of more come to me,
My family, friends, and others.
Encouraging, supporting, and holding me accountable.
Feeling like the trees reaching for the sky,
Accomplished and proud doing anything I desire,
Choosing to influence others and help them become better people.

THE LAUREL HILL SCHOOL
Tricia Lomando-Bird

 # Honorable Mentions

The Open Road of No Stress
Brendan Doyle

You leave all your stress and your worries behind,
There is an open road,
You feel better about yourself,
You aren't stressed therefore you are happy,
There is an open road,
You aren't worried therefore you are stress free,
There is an open road,
You have no pressure therefore you are mellow,
There is an open road,
You have no anxiety therefore you are composed,
On this journey you are calm,
You relax and have fun,
You walk through a calm forest,
You hear birds chirping and the wind blowing,
You are pleased and stay for a while,
As you sit, you look around you at birds and trees,
There is an open road,
With endless things to do,
And finally you are stress and worry free.

TUCKAHOE COMMON MIDDLE SCHOOL
Alison Goldberg

Where I Want to Go
Cathleen Annello

I wish the road was smooth;
If only it was easy.
I looked for shortcuts and
lights to guide me.
But there were none.

The road was long
And there were so many bumps along the way.
The drive was boring, and every driver was impatient with the traffic.

Butterflies filled my stomach, and I could not eat a bite of food.
The drive seemed to take forever in the stifling heat.
I prayed that we would get there on time.

Little by little, we inched toward our destination.
The buildings were tall and gray, unwelcoming.
My mouth felt dry and my voice felt lost.
But there was no time to worry.

The clicking of the cameras brought me back to life.
The fluttering in my stomach disappeared.
I smiled, and I posed.
I was in my element.

And even though this is my first time
It feels like I've come home...

ST. DOMINIC ELEMENTARY
Ana Bifulco

Golden Hour
Emily Gravitz

The sun glows in the sky.
The gravel road stretches out
to the farthest corners of the planet.
I hear the click clack of my shoes as I leap forward.
I dance in the sunlight. My hands are golden.
The golden hour is upon us.

A golden breeze flies around me as I dance into the garden.
I see the roses blooming into imperfect, abstract shapes.
The roses smell fresh and bright. Bees fly, pollinating flowers.
My hair flies in the wind. The wind brushes my cheek.
I smell the fragrant lilies, the white lilies like fresh fruit.
I glimpse the white lilies beneath the roses. The sky begins to darken.

I catch a last glimpse of the sun. I hear creatures scurrying
back to their homes. The road is empty, eerie, a ghost town.
During the day, there are so many people talking in their houses.
Now, in the silence, I remember all the stories I've heard.
I remember your stories about friendship. I remember your smile
when you showed me photographs of your friends laughing. I remember

the sun in the sky smiling as we laughed together.
Then I remember how many people's stories remain untold,
all the people who kept silent. I remember the sorrow in their eyes.
I shared with them my stories of love, and their eyes glowed.
But I also shared with them my stories of hardship,
and their eyes began to darken again.

They all hugged me goodbye because we all knew
that soon I would have to leave and continue my adventure,
but there is one person I will never leave.
I turn around and offer you my hand.
Together we will choose our path,
traversing the universe.

Category B, Individual Poem Grades 5–6
LAKEVILLE ELEMENTARY SCHOOL
Colleen O'Sullivan

The Joys of Travel
Grace Jones

I love to travel
I love the sunsets on the beach
I love going on the lifeguard chairs that I can barely reach
I love looking at mountains too big to climb
I love trying new drinks, on the rim there's a lime
The wind in my hair, the sun in my face
Every bad thing seems to be erased
My toes in the sand
Looking at the new lands
Every new place I go, my heart expands
Every time I travel, a good time is guaranteed
I guess you could say that travel is all I need

HOLY CHILD ACADEMY
Mrs. DeLuca

No Other Way for Me
Noora Ahmed

I will go to the farthest lengths in search of my road.
Not everyone's road is fit for others.
Sometimes one's road is only for them.

My road is a place with memorable scents and looks.
The journey to my road may not be perfect.
But the end of the road is perfect for me.

My road is not straight.
There are bumps and turns along the way.
Only one way will lead to the end.

My road is a place with a sound to calm one's body.
The journey to my road will change between light and dark.
My road will start and end the way it's supposed to.

As time goes by,
As others look for their road,
My road continues to grow with what I have picked up along the way.

Failure will lengthen my road.
Success will lengthen my road.
I will control my road with what I have learned.

No one else is supposed to go down your road.
Only you.

The Foggy Road
Janae Henry

The road ahead is foggy, and the ground is awfully soggy
And though I cannot see,
I shall continue going.
The road straight ahead, is made for more than one
How about you and I move along together

And as you walk it may get you a little groggy
But just know the foggy road is not just the journey
It's what you carry and how you carry it
Across the unclear valley.

The foggy road is very cold, but it will pass in months
It sounds long
But trust me the wait is worth it all
One day the fog will lift, and you will have to go.

Enjoy it with what you have left
And think nothing of the end
Just remember how you spent it and who you made your friend.
The road is getting clear now
The light is quickly shifting
Soon you'll begin to see.
How does it feel to get through a challenge on this foggy road with me?

Careful! It's a setback
Don't let it downgrade your pride
Hold up your head and think clearly to keep up your stride
On this foggy road with me.
We need to push through
However, whatever we go through
Do not let your ego grow too much
It will slow you down so much

The foggy road is at an end
Nice to know you - see you next journey, my friend.

Category B, Individual Poem Grades 5–6
THE LAUREL HILL SCHOOL
Tricia Lomando-Bird

Towards the Ever Blazing Sun
Oorja Anand Singh

A twisting road lay before me,
Battered and worn from the travels set upon it,

But proudly did it march towards the ever blazing sun,
With determination such that I had in myself,

As I realized how far I could go.

Would go.

If I learned from my mistakes,
And learned from others' mistakes,

If I looked at the light when there was dark,
And helped the dark find light as well,

If I was not blinded by my own lies,
But could take off the blindfold if there was one,

If I let those who would help me do just that,
And gave those who needed help just that.

With these thoughts swirling like a mighty storm through my head,
Words of insight and courage and beauty striking lightning,

I stood my ground upon the valiant grassless patch that stretched before me,
One inspired foot in front of the other,

Knowing in my bones that all of the journeys made across this road were true,
And maybe just as exotic and new as mine could be,

But also that each step I took would light in me a fire so unique,
One that no one else could feel engulfed with,

One that may even end up fueling the greatest good this road has ever seen,
Or that could set a never ceasing darkness upon my path.

I set upon this road, an ocean of possibilities that it had never seen before,

So, proudly did I march towards the ever blazing sun,
On this twisting road that lay before me.

ROSLYN MIDDLE SCHOOL

On the Old Valley
Parnav Chadha

As I see the lights of day
Coming of morning on the road
As hope for the trip to end
As the deathly heat comes in
I start to daydream about the beaches
Back home on the Long Island road
As I feel the steering wheel
Driving into the desert road
As I touch the gear and put it in drive
As I hope to see the Las Vegas sky
As the tire start burning with the bad smell
As the blue sky becomes shy
As times change by the hour
Death Valley sand with its danger beneath it
As we come half way
To the city of the state
With the hope of the grim heat
To be gone but as I know the heat never goes away
As the cold isn't here
As the city comes up
I see the sign of the end
As the quote "as hope for the trip to end" fades away
As I enter the city of hotels
With the exit sign to the right
As I pull into the city
As I grab the gear into park
As I walk out from the heat
As I see him standing there
With his name
Dwayne Johnson on his name tag.

BURNS AVENUE SCHOOL
Alison Urkiel

Farther
Weizheng Evalyn Chen

My arms are heavy from hours of rowing.

The salt-seasoned air of the ocean rises.

Just ahead, my parents glide in a splish-splash momentum

of blue waves. With rhythm, droplets hit my face, fat water

obscuring my vision. The brisk cold wind blows the rain.

My sandaled feet are submerged in a pool. Below me,

an octopus passes by, dark ink camouflaging itself.

A sandy mountain ahead seems like miles, each row getting me closer.

But each row, the sand seems farther. An ache begins

at my fingers, then passes through my heart to my shoulders.

My knees huddle in, away from a dark blue eel, the spots surrounded by a
halo of light blue. It slips between sharp edges of coral that look like flowers.

My parents have reached land, their silhouettes are black dots.

I spot two hands waving at me and I squeeze the paddle harder,

squinting through heavy rain, thinking how hard this journey is alone.

A vast sea spreads across many miles eroding with colors

Warmth washes over me like a hug at the end of a long day as I paddle

across, closing the distance between my boat and my parents.

Category B, Individual Poem Grades 5–6
WEST LAFAYETTE INTERMEDIATE SCHOOL
Mrs. Stan

INDIVIDUAL POEM, GRADES 7 & 8

Category C

Grand Champion 1st Place

In Hopes of Finding Myself Once More
Shreya Satpathy

I, the child, in the blossoming park

I take a whiff of each velvety flower bud, letting the smell waft in
I always eat and I eat, every sweet, every savory delight
My hands are messy, but I have an unfaltering grin
I dance in the sunlight, underneath every soaring kite's flight
Every day is bright, from dawn till dark

I, the painter, on the long open road
Creating new worlds, sprouting new truth
I paint and paint, art galore
Trying to find ephemeral inner peace and beauty, although I am still in my youth
Colors always mix into unsure shades of black, and brown, and grey; beauty is never forevermore
Brush strokes and colors are no longer my humble abode

I, the musician, at the gentle pianoforte
Day and night, the nonstop singing
Weaving melodies and harmonies by song,
Every emotion, opinion, every piece of my being
But now my melody falters, its tune long gone,
My spirit demure, lost in the cacophony.

I, the actress, in the empty theatre
Every day, the same old game
I will wear a thousand faces and pretend to be anyone:
A fighter, a dreamer, an adventurer, a dame
In that crowd of thousands I would love to be one
But how can I express who I am, if I am yet to meet her?

Recently, I have come to envy that innocent child
I have strayed from my true self, dwelling too long on scars
Now I must journey, with no one but myself for company
And I wish to wander back to when I had time to admire the stars
I will wander endlessly
In hope to someday find myself once more, even if it takes a while

Category C, Individual Poem Grades 7–8
W.T. CLARKE MIDDLE SCHOOL
Mrs. Dale

They Call Her Liberty
Ziya Yin

Told to be independent yet patronized. We
come to escape,
for what the founding father promised. We
come here to be free,
yet find ourselves trapped under more chains than we ever were. They
call it the land of opportunities.
The yellow light which shines from the hand of the fair lady, a
beacon of hope, liberty, freedom.
the same light that shone from the factories,
the same light our kind labored under in the mines,
the same light that our children hopelessly study through the night with, hoping
to escape the grasps of a meaningless, mundane life.
Tell me, why do humans take this path for freedom, yet
they fight tooth and nail for just a sliver, a taste. I am one
of those children.

Grand Champion 3rd Place

A One-Way Journey
Stephanie Green

They say, "life's a journey, not a destination"
and I wholly agree,
My road doesn't lead to nowhere–
there's a reason why I'm alive
And I can't just take up space.

My road isn't perfect
There are deep cracks in the asphalt
And potholes and bumps
It's not always smooth sailing.

On my road I pass by lush forests filled with singing birds
And the warm sun is smiling at me
Filling me with hope for what's to come.

But my road travels through deserts, too
That wring out all my energy
As if I were a towel,
and hope was the water.

My road depends on my decisions
and they are inspired by my parents,
loved ones around me
And the lessons I've learned on the way.

My road is one-way,
I cannot relive any parts of my life
nor fix past mistakes
It is what it is.

There are brief moments when I feel like my road
Is going in circles
And I'm not getting anywhere
But I know that God is helping me
Get to the end of my road
So I can rejoice with Him in heaven

For all eternity.

30 *Category C, Individual Poem Grades 7–8*
   MOUNT SINAI MIDDLE SCHOOL
   Ryneld Curtis

 ## Honorable Mentions

Storm
Alexa Surdi

Glass floor, white road,
Thunder cracks, the sun shows
One person, two roads.
"Go," commands the stormy red beach.
"Stay," welcomes the beautiful blue skies.
My better conscience tells me to follow the angelic voice that beckons me
Into the blue skied meadow, but my mind has other plans.
Brave the storm.

Charging into the demonic sight, crack, thunder booms, crack, I continue forward, crack.
The glass shatters, leaving the coarse sand in a toss up with shards of clear knives.
I will continue on.
The red sea rages as the swells hit my feet.
It burns, I fall, it burns, I scream, it burns. I look into the sky.
One singular star hovering all alone in a blood sky whispers to me.
"The path you are on is a strong one, you must
Brave the storm."

I rise, glass ripping at my hands and feet, but I don't feel pain.
A walk turns to a jog, a jog to a run, and a run to a sprint.
I continue, the red storm progressively getting worse.
The tides grow restless, and the winds infuriate.
I run for hours, but I'm not tired.
Faster and faster and faster I go.
Brave the storm.

The world goes black as I collapse, but instead of the glassy sand concoction
I feel smooth sand on my face.
Birds sing, the sky is blue, as the salty breeze coats my lungs.
The world around me is still and peaceful at last.
I braved the storm.

Category C, Individual Poem Grades 7–8
MOUNT SINAI MIDDLE SCHOOL
Nicole Wallace

Dense Air
Ariel Ruggiero

Lift off

In my true element

Uncaged by the norm,

Free like a soaring blue jay looking for its inner peace,

The clouds elevate me towards a higher being

Fill my whole being,

With delight.

As I increase my elevation,

The dense air moving in rapidly from the north,

Below the crashing waves on the coast

Bursting with new beginnings,

The depth of the sea is blue and clear,

Her eyes

My heart skips a beat even way up here

I feel an emptiness as I felt before

Like our last night together,

Purity like a wind caressing

Over a thousand meadows of wildflowers, Up

high in the north country,

The ocean is no longer in sight,

And her essence has gone.

My aircraft bends and struggles over the dense air

My wings difficult to keep level

I keep pressure on the joystick

Clear skies above the horizon

I head due east towards the morning light,

Montauk light

Crisp orange light

Kisses the horizon

A new day is near

SPRINGS SCHOOL
Emily O'Reilly

Colors Of The Open Road
Evelyn Saunders

The cobblestone clacks as I take my first step.
A familiar pull tugs me relentlessly along the road, calling to my dreams, my hopes.
My hands never rest, my mind a constant whirlwind as I cross the land.
From this day forward, I vow to not wait for my moment, instead seizing every second,
weaving inspiration throughout the world like grains of sand through an hourglass.
I charge over the trail, blazing a path, until I hear a song.
The voices of family, of love and peaceful lives call over the wind,
Dancing laughter, the warmth of a hearth, they sing a melody all their own.
They follow me wherever I travel, whispering to a soft yearning in my heart.
I pause.
I close my eyes, and for a fleeting moment, simply listen.
I listen, and I feel, and I smell, and I open my eyes.
There's the slosh of water in a riverbed, the crack of a stick under a deer's hoof.
The cool, sharp sensation of the first raindrop on my face, followed by a torrent
The smells of nature, of the forest after a storm.
The scent of my firewood, wafting into the sky.
My arms spread wide, I embrace the day, with its rise and fall, its darkness and light.
On my journey, I hear stories, listen to people, cry and laugh along with those I encounter.
But with each new thread of connection, each new design, comes a goodbye.
Behind me trail thousands of strings and thoughts and memories,
Forming something completely new.
And with every fall of the day, I lay next to my fire,
Surrounded by my world full of stories to be discovered.
I see the sky's great canvas, stretching for miles.
Painted with passionate reds, piercing blues, and reflective pinks,
All fading into dark, introspective black.
And on that open road, the path I have carved,
I sit content to continue until my tale comes to an end, until I reach the end of the road,
And the source of my song.

FRIENDS ACADEMY
Adriana Bocchino

Belly of the Beast
Gianna Fitzpatrick

The moon winks to me tauntingly,
my last wink of slumber, moons ago.

Gleaming ivory columns curl northward,
guiding the way towards an uncertain destination.

I breathe,
seemingly alongside this cavern,
as I lie and tell myself I'm aware of what lies ahead.

The wet bones of exotic animals
watch me,
as they wait for this weary woman to waltz with fate.

I tremble in pure, raw, unadulterated fear.

My eyes are unwillingly observing
the blood caked on to the blanch stalagmites,
and the putrid water droplets plunging
from the sinewy ceiling.
Yet I remind myself of the purpose of this journey.

The people I have left at home count on me,

for my kingdom's civilians live in fear
of the tyrannical drake that soars above.
He blocks out their light with his mighty red wings.

I recall the kin of my kith,
who could not wait to kill such a creature.

Alas, he was swiftly silenced.

Nay, I shan't suffer the same grisly defeat.

I shan't allow such a beast to roar louder than I.

What I shall do,
is I shall strike it down and bring freedom to my people's oppression.

I vow to pierce its treacherous gut.

So I will myself further, guarded only by my wits and faith.

So I will myself further, down into the belly of the beast.

Category C, Individual Poem Grades 7–8
WANTAGH MIDDLE SCHOOL
Christine Hult

My Forged Path
Janis Fok

A bright road illuminated by radiant signs lies ahead of me,
The road that may alter the world,
The road that awaits my tread.

Light without burden,
as how birds soar across blue skies, I firmly grasp my sign,
A formidable weapon that long anticipated my touch,
A weapon led by a relentless crowd chanting in unison.

Once I raise my sign high enough, I chase a dream,
a dream to transform this world, even by a bit,
even if I wasn't the only one.

The puddles of rain and mud lie beneath me, as if to hinder me,
as if to let everything be.

The route of freedom,
the coastline that faded to white to green to blue, the
two yellow lines that seem to expand endlessly, Then the
tears that trickled down my cheeks.

Even if the rain drenched my clothes,
Even if the road never ceases,
Even if I had a silent voice,

I will forge a path.

GREAT NECK SOUTH MIDDLE SCHOOL
Mrs. Marr

The Journey of Life
Nicole Kolasny

Upon this open road I tread,
A world of wonder lies ahead.
The blacktop whispers underneath my feet,
A symphony of journey sweet.

No map or compass in my hand,
Just wanderlust and dreams so grand.
Each mile a story is yet untold,
A memory to have and hold.

The skyline paints a canvas new,
In shades of pink, orange, and blue.
The road, a friend who knows no end,
Around each bend, a new amend.

The stars above, my guiding light,
They glimmer with a traveler's delight.
The moon, a beacon in the night,
Illuminates the road so right.

Within every town, a fresh greeting,
To strangers who may come and go.
We share a moment, then we part,
Each leaving footprints on the heart.

So let us travel without fear,
For every end is just near.

The open road calls out my name,
To play its endless game.

I'll answer with a heart so bold,
For life is best on roads untold.
When my journey meets its close,
I'll find the remain of where the road goes.

Category C, Individual Poem Grades 7–8
ST. AIDAN SCHOOL
Mrs. Fanning

Untitled
Nora Aziz

Crying and moody, how I enter this temporary world,
But as soon as you hold me, I bawl no more,
Whilst I threw my tantrums, you found a way to make me at ease,
You cradled me in your arms,
Fed me your own milk,
Tied my shoes every time,
Cooked your nutritious and mostly delicious meals for me,
Dropped me off at school every day,
Picked me up from school every day,
Did my hair every day,
Suddenly I felt like I didn't need you anymore,
Aggravated and agitated every time you try to "baby" me,
Annoyed of everything you tell me to do,
As my journey continues, I see that you were right,
Smothered me with love, but I take it for granted,
You fed me 5 star meals while you ate leftovers,
You styled my hair while yours was a mess,
Bought me new clothes while you wore old clothes,
Uncertain of where the road takes me,
But I know for certain I want you in it

NEW HYDE PARK MEMORIAL HIGH SCHOOL
Mrs. K. Kaspar

NORTH WIND
Patrick Baynon

The fragrant, snow-covered evergreens were beautiful
on the icy tundra
I could feel the wisps of snow on my brow
away from civilization without a care in the world

I was liberated of the criticism and my responsibilities, I was free

My will to travel has taken me here to the cold Canadian wilderness, I am at
    peace as I
stare forth at what awaits my arrival
who awaits my arrival
part of my mind dreads this journey out of worry of
what may lie ahead
but I will embrace whatever happens to me whether it's good or
detrimental

I will continue this adventure
getting to know my only companion out here, myself

HOLY CHILD ACADEMY
Kristina DeLuca

Through a path with...
Pinar Isildak

from the very beginning
from the youngest ages
from the start of the path
hidden deep inside
so **S**ilent so far

they have a de**E**p feeling
of love
of hate
of guilt

i need to speak
i need to tell
"so hard to keep inside"

They take over my mind, my path
It will set me off course
in the middle of the night
in my nightmares
they s**C**ream
they kill
to be set f**R**ee

no one can see them
no one will admit them
but w**E** all have them
each worse
each deeper than the nex**T**

til the very end
they stay
til the day i breath my last
til the end of the twi**S**ted path

The Closed Road
Sara Martella

Optimistic, yet nervous, I take the
closed road I am here, I see
opportunity
A cobblestone road, my head goes there

Opportunities to work hard for
success To carry my feet along
To think with my heart
I want to be new to this road

This closed road is time
Seeping through my fingers
like water A familiar sound as it
hits the road Tick Tock, Tick
Tock, Tick
Waiting for me
I cannot accept time

My feet endure each bump
The leaves change me as they
change I smell my deepest
desires
The end is not in reach, not yet

The road is closed to those who accept
barriers I have changed myself as I
have the road Barreling through the
barrier
A closed road is closed to the ones who do not leave the car

ST. DOMINIC ELEMENTARY AND MIDDLE SCHOOL
Ana Bifulco

Shards
Yuri Montas

They come to the open road with situations like glass shards,
Awaiting the day when their jaguars come to roar out their cries before me,
As I wait patiently for the time to tick by.

They feel the road as a burst of color,
Yet I am bound with chains to the ground; suppressed by faults,
Deep wounds surround me; my approachers asking my name,
But I give them a kiss of light.

As time passes by, the world unfolds,
All of its seams unraveling before me—few and far between,
Yet I am like a patchwork quilt, never finished, yet always done.

I search and pry more, into *their* life,
Men and women, elder and eldest, modest beyond the stars,
However, may they stay the same, like a blooming rose,
And may they cast their thorns to the road, saying:

"Hark! Take heed, let not themselves be affiliated with you and me,
Let them not clasp you into their hands,
For you are yours to sculpt."

As the end draws nearer, and *they* take their final moments,
As a seeming eternal clock fails to tick, and the jaguars—yes, their persecutors
sullen, I am left to bear witness for all the things I've seen,
But I choose to stay as the road, until *they* come again.

INDIVIDUAL POEM, GRADES 9 & 10

Category D

Grand Champion 1st Place

Grass
Jacob Torczyner

What had once been just a strip of barren land turned to nature
It said, "Oh, how painful it is to be a blank slate.
Please show me mercy and allow me to grow."
In return nature replied, "Though you are now nothing, you will become great as the roads of Rome."

It was after 9 months that this prophecy of sorts came to light.
The clean-shaven road had sprouted a blade of grass.
Yet this was no ordinary grass, this was grass shaped like a newborn.
The road looked in awe as, slowly, the grass arose, and three more blades surrounded it.
One was a mother, another a father, and the final one a young boy.

Over time the grass morphed into a young lad, ready to face the world.
In his hands were a book of great significance and a pencil.
The boy looked over the book for days upon end as the road looked on.
Then he started to write.
He was not picky as to the surface he wrote on, all that mattered were the words.

Soon enough the road was covered in words and human-shaped grass, a hub of life and thoughts prime for growth.
Some of the grass blades helped the boy while a few others tried to push him down.
But one thing was certain to the boy.
He wanted to write.

Time passed, papyrus paper piled sky-ward like a mountain slated with snow-like words.
The once young boy was now a man, ready to move to bigger roads.
He carried with him his paper and said his farewells to the road.
Then, he became detached from the earth and floated on. Some followed him, others stayed but the grass went by.

Even though the sun and moon passed by thousands of times, the road remembered the child.
The indentation that was left in it was a remembrance for generations.

Category D, Individual Poem Grades 9–10
DAVIS RENOV STAHLER YESHIVA HIGH SCHOOL FOR BOYS
Joseph DeMarco

The Winding Path
Allen Sinai

Pedaling fast on this open road, under skies so vast and blue,
My bike and I, a single force, cutting the air in two.
Through streets that stretch to endless lands, where adventures hide,
I ride through whispers of the trees, the wind my faithful guide.
The taste of adrenaline, mixed with the dust of trails,

As I dodge through shadows and light, my spirit never fails.
This bike, my escape, from a world too tight and confined,
Here, on these open roads, a new perspective I find.
I chose this path for the thrill, for the challenge it presents,
Every hill and every curve, my resolve it represents.

Obstacles, they come and go, like the hills that rise and fall,
But with every push and pedal, I feel I can conquer them all.
So I pedal on, with heart light and eyes wide,
Embracing every moment of this exhilarating ride.
For on this road, with wheels spinning, in the silence or the din,
I find my freedom, my joy, in the wind against my skin.

Arboraceous Wanderer
William Pereira

I see a moss-laden path under a sorrowful sky,
a crow and a dove tempt my path, I ignore them.
I see what looms over the trees and their pungent, lovely mist,
however faintly, obstructed by the trees, I see.
Shrouded in the crashing waves of thought, it lies before me;
It is distant, it is obscured, it is beautiful.
I am pushed back by the wind and forward by my will:
Am I the eye in this storm?
Lilacs yearn at my heels, and crumble foolishly under my feet.
I see them not, I only hope to catch a glimpse beyond the trees.
A fawn crosses before me, and I allow myself to be guided,
beyond the fir sea; beyond my path.
It appears before me in my recollection,
a path, moss-laden and morose.
I long for its end, but crave its faint earthy scent.
I ache for the clearing in the trees, and I yearn to see,
and I walk through the trees, led by the fawn.
Ah, such beauty in these trees.

 Honorable Mentions

Unbound

Alexis Thomas

I tread paths on dirt and dust
The earth's patterns swirl with every step
The trees whisper guides, offering their wisdom
Each branch points me in a new direction

I yearn to see what the world has to offer
Feel the unfelt and touch the untouched
My senses hum absorbing the crisp scents of nature
Fragrant flowers...cool breeze...warm soil

The fields began to look like a constellation; so many places, such little time
This path of learning threads through the mountains of doubt
It passes the valleys of uncertainty
The right path will lead to bliss

With time, everything will fall into place
Just as the raindrops fall onto the earth's surface
The beauty of the earth is a mystery waiting to be revealed
My quest remains boundless; a dreamer ready to step into the unknown

My Road Is Me
AnaLuz Ferrer

My road is a winding pathway,
with loops and zigzags and tunnels and
turns. My road contains the dos and the
don'ts,
The yeses and the nos,
That I have obtained from the people and experiences of
my life. My road is who I was,
Who I am now,
And who I strive to be.
My road shows a little girl,
Coloring and reading children's books in
preschool. My road shows a 9th grader,
Trying to figure out what she wants to do with her life--who she wants to be.
My road shows a future Architect,
Striving for greatness and living her life to the
fullest. My road is being paved as we speak,
Each brick a
decision, Each stone
an event. As I grow,
My road grows.
As I live,
My road lives.
As I move forward in life, my road follows.
My road...is me.

Category D, Individual Poem Grades 9–10
OYSTER BAY HIGH
Ms. Murphy

Hello
Giuliana DePaola

I'm sorry that I'm leaving,
Just know this is not goodbye;
It is a thousand new hellos
Underneath the same old sky.

I will see so many things, I have never known before,
Which is why in my heart, I know I must explore.

I will say hello to the mountains, and the strength within their rocks,
I will say hello to the ocean, and the boats along the docks,
I will say hello to new creatures, ones that play and run amok,
I will say so many hellos that I don't know when I'll stop.

I will say hello to new people, and hear the way they talk,
I want to learn about their lives, and the streets down which they walk,
I want to hear their music, maybe play some of their games,
I want to see what's different, and bond over what's the same.

There are countless tiny worlds
Underneath this bright blue sky,
There are so many more who live under it
Than simply you and I.

So do not say goodbye to me,
As I pack my things and go—
Because maybe in the future,
We can once again say hello.

Story Of My Life
Grace Kuskowski

My road is a song, it has endless possibilities
It can be happy, it can be sad
In the start it's loud, and ends in silence
My road is an ocean, it knows no bounds
It is free as a bird,
but can strike like a bull
My road is a field of flowers, it's so beautiful.
I walk around the thorns and bees, focusing on not getting hurt
I have never gotten hurt from thorns and bees, but I'm still careful
My road is a bed, there for me from morning to night
Soft and comfortable, it holds me close and keeps me warm
My road is a snowy mountain,
So beautiful but holds so much danger
Never go down it alone
My road sings to me, the song of life.
It shows me the sights only I can see
It can be an ocean, it can be a field of flowers
It can be a snowy mountain, or my own bed
My road smells warm, cold, floral, cozy
It smells like all places I call home
My road tastes salty, sweet, cold, warm
Each reminding me where I began, where I am headed
My road feels like home
No matter the weather I will always find a family
My road sounds like everything
It sings not one song, but a new one each day
Every day is a new road I travel down, every song tells a different story
All of these paths are different, they are there for different reasons
All to help me and teach me
And they all sing the story of my life.

The Ballad of Footsteps
Isabella Fernandim

Darkness, decorated by the tapping of heels
The music of uncertainty
Tap, tap, tap
The ballad of each footstep balancing the weight of a girl
Symbolizing the nerving decision of moving forward

Rocks, once the steady stepping stones of my ancestors
Pulverized through each dream down our family tree
Treading through the soil, my feet kick up a haze of lost memories

A waft of nostalgia, the scent of the ocean's breeze lingers through the air
The sound of my grandmother's voice calling behind
Her lullaby faintly being sung between palm trees

The background of my journey adorned with the ebbing of the sea

Sunflowers planted in my father's garden

Sunny side up, the taste of my mother's mornings

My heart, always pulsing back towards the comfort of childhood
Fifteen years of tracks, I run thirty steps back to the promise of youth
Back to the promise of hiding under quilts with love sewn into each thread

Yet, I fail to match my footsteps
Tripping on my childhood shoelaces
The red string unravels in front of me
Forming the labyrinth of the future
My heart, beating forward in search of a newfound purpose

In letting go of past generations, I yearn for the possibility of future history
No longer carrying their baggage, I put on my mother's scuffed shoes
Each scratch, once a witness to the trial of every diverging road
The pattern of her soles perfectly matching the footsteps ahead of me
Her memory, a compass guiding me through every twist and turn
My destination, not tethered to the place I once called home
But the love I find in every winding path I roam

Category D, Individual Poem Grades 9–10

SACRED HEART ACADEMY
Allison Mertz

Echoes of Abandoned Dreams
Madison Bruck

The barren road is covered in fallen brown leaves and wasted possibilities

The tires of my car screech on the wet terrain I drive down

Sounding as if they were pleading with me to turn around

Yet I ignore the pleas to stop

My car jolts as it runs over a muddy pothole

A beeping noise floods my ears

Low air pressure, yet my spirit refuses to give up

Nevertheless I still ignore the warnings

A fallen tree has struck the road from the storm

I see no barrier, so I continue my journey

The road I am most familiar with is wrapped in neon tape screaming caution

I turn the beaten steering wheel to the left

I distance myself from the familiar ties that once bounded me

In the chaos, I find my spirit yearning to explore

The road widens as the smell of salt and seaweed fills the empty air

The gleaming sky of shades of red, orange, and pink reflect off the foggy side view mirrors

With the fallen leaves and wasted possibilities behind me

The road ahead is now open

Journey of the Open Road
Matilda Saltiel

At times I trudge on a barren road
Before me: a cracked and desolate land
Still, I make the trek and hold the knowledge that
it will pass. Rather, I will pass it

At times I skip on a vibrant road
Passing bustling markets and lively chatter
I hold the knowledge of those I meet,
and grant them access to my secrets too

As I walk, I paint murals of the people I have known
Beautiful colors, shades of gray
I paint with the hope that someday,
somewhere, I will see a painting made for me

I will stop and I will stare
I will know that I have touched lives
I will look, and I will look away
I will keep walking on my road: my path to the future

I will stroll, I will guide
I will wander, I will hike
I will always be moving
Be searching for the next step on my road

At all times, I walk on a road
My road: overlapping and crisscrossing and winding
And I know, no matter where I go
My road will lead me home

The Road of Life
Sebastian Song

The road of life is often difficult

A winding path, challenges left and right
Throughout it all, each step tells a story
An intricate tale, a wonder of itself

Through twists and turns, we navigate
Facing the struggles that stand along
Companions join, their presence guides
Together we walk, side by side.

Obstacles rise, like mountains to climb
Defeats, like valleys in our path
Through the mountainous terrain, we grow
Learning and developing, result of win and defeat

The journey of life, though difficult

Builds one's skills, no

It builds a person, It shapes their ways
It's what makes you who you are

Nature's Road
Thomas Matranga

Flakes of ice produce an endless sea of white,
The merciless area blows wind into my face.
A vast forest of birchwood trees encompass the area,
The road is blind to most as I travel,
With only glints of red lighting my path,
and crevices of pushed-in snow.
Nothing can be heard but the billowing of the wind,
The naked branches of the trees cannot dance,
And the songbirds of the forest hide in fear.
I find tranquility in the grey clouds of the sky,
As the shadows illustrate my sickle,
And my boots break the peace.
Soon thereafter I discover a rock,
Encircled in its surrounding is glistening red.
And in my gaze I find my pity,
And in its gaze it finds my mercy,
As the shuddering noise shakes my road.
But I stand tall in its wake,
Order has once again been kept,
And the price of my survival is received.

Retrace
Veronica Qui

Leaving the loud thoughts behind me,
l hop onto my beige Townie bike
and let my feet sink into the pedals.
I ride the rumble over the train tracks,
petrichor emanating from the road
where the trees arch over the street
and a flute melody seeps through the
open windows of a cabin house.
Puffs of warm air form with every exhale
while I make my way down Middlefield.
For miles, I clench cuffs tightly over my knuckles,
preventing waves of chilliness from entering.
Flickering, my bike lights make the road ahead
barely visible. I reach the pedestrian bridge
over the buzzing highway, but I'm not yet ready to cross.
I turn back and retrace my original path.
I squiggle through the dim suburbs,
pots scurrying, lights whispering, and living room clamoring
is where I stop. The doormat welcomes me home.
I kick my shoes off and find my seat next to Grandpa.
The dinner table's steam inflates the whole house.
Chopsticks fly over the bowl of freshly steamed egg,
the daunting redness of mapo tofu,
and the cooked salad soaking in its own broth.
Our laughter reverberates through the walls.
We'll slouch onto the couch together
and watch a Chinese drama
about a large family living in one house,
the warm food sitting in our stomachs,
full as bloated balloons.

INDIVIDUAL POEM, GRADES 11 & 12

Category E

Grand Champion 1st Place

4:00 AM Tuesdays at the Airport
Jiwan Kim

My father always bought tickets
When no one else wished to go places.

Heavy-eyed TSA agents,
Beaten down by the fluorescent lights,
Weren't as worried about sweaty palms or
The sneakers I'd accidentally left on.

My father and I parted from their forced company
Into the deserted terminal.

I tip-toed through the rectangular hallway,
Fearing I would disrupt this theater without an audience.
This mall without customers.
This sky without clouds.

The woman doused in drab business attire and weighed down
By eyebags simpered as she flipped through
The cardstock pages of *The Rainbow Fish*.
And my father, scanning through his work files,
Enjoyed a refreshing room-temperature Coors Light
Paired with his favorite blue jelly-beans.

The silence of the lemon-scented disinfectant
The janitor wiped on the seats,
The tingling cold hurrying from the vents,
The smoothly operating metal escalator
Drumming on through the night,
The absence of feet on the desire path
Worn into the carpet by dragging heels, boots, and flip-flops.
4:00 AM Tuesday at the airport
Was the quietest.

So I cartwheeled down the desolate path.
And my giggles echoed
Into the depths of the dreary terminal.

Category E, Individual Poem Grades 11–12
HORACE MANN SCHOOL
Richard Weems

Grand Champion 2nd Place

anatomy of a hodophile
Rina Olsen

> *And that is the reason we're on this road.*
> — Orpheus, *Hadestown*

what reason need there be when the body is the road. i pedal
   on wheels of irises, sprockets framing my pupils in place so i won't

have to look away. the broken GPS in my skull keeps sending me to
   ghost towns but i can still find beauty in refusing to give up the road

to the stars. i pedal along my vertebrae railroad in time to the metronome
   of the steam engine, pedaling towards the doctor's stethoscope. the cold

fingerprint on my map to see if the road is still mine. i slide my feet from
   the straps to free-fall past the cherry-blossom tree my tongue is hewn from.

between my tonsils, the crashing boulders of Odysseus. past the oil fields
   of my tastebuds where ink & constellations pump to the surface. down

into the voicebox of summer saturated with soda dreams & bare feet
   on pavement. i look for this road. i look for the ghosts walking it:

the crossing guard, the woman with the calamansi tree, the salt-encrusted
   boots by the radiator. *we don't know where we're going either*, they signed,

but we'll get there eventually. Orpheus, i tried. i tried like you tried. my
   ribs, strung with the same IV lines of your lyre but i'm playing this journey

by ear and can you blame me? with each correct note / footstep, looking
   over my shoulder to see if i was actually blessed. i jump off the bike when

i reach the mercy of a cartographer's compass and hammer my body
   into a runway of adrenaline from the seam where Atlantic meets Pacific.

i look for this road. for stop signs bent over with migraines, for the
   patina marking my hip bones. i look for myself and only let myself stop

when i reach the heart. carefully, so as not to hurt, i crawl into my
   aorta. and breathe. it fogs before my lips to tell me that i am alive. i

listen in silence. i listen to the thump-thump-thump of my heart, the thumping
   of each footstep and this bicycle has banked on the side but it is still beautiful

in its laurels of rust. how beautiful for a human heart to sound like a road's
   lifeline. how beautiful for this human heart to be mine, and this road's lifeline me.

Category E, Individual Poem Grades 11–12

ST. JOHN'S SCHOOL
Tiana King

Onions
Damaris Sumba Lliguin

Mom's cooking something in the kitchen,
I'm not sure what, but in mind I know it's good.
Paprika, garlic, onions,
The last one made the tears in my eyes sting, The
onions remind me of the troubles,
The troubles I deal with in life, Moments
where I would weep to myself.

That's when I would look up front;
Look up and not see the clear road ahead. For so
long I didn't know which road to take.
Relatives, friends, giving me different directions, To
roads that to them sounded right for me.
Sometimes those roads are tangled up in a mess, Like
the mess I have in me.
If not onions like what my mom uses,
Are what causes tears, then it might as well, Be
life itself.

Although now as I head my into final year of school,
My senses seem to navigate.
The roads that were tangled still seem as tangled. But this
time I decided on something new,
That I have to make my own path,
Pave the way for it.
Now as I find the way to this new path,

The onions don't sting as much.
I still feel it, though it is now bearable.
When I see my mother in the kitchen,
I think of the struggles of the immigrants and her,
How they built this new road for us,
At now what I'll be doing too.

Category E, Individual Poem Grades 11–12
BELLPORT HIGH SCHOOL
Sarah Emma

 # Honorable Mentions

i am free jazz
Andrew Fogel

we travel it's carved out path, from the first note to the last
breathing in paper
give the paper my soul I shall, and guidance it will give me in return
the paper becoming a vessel, a conductor
for the orchestra of myself.

forte can carry a curious whisper
c major a canvas yet to be colored
nothing more than a mentor I try
to vanquish with vibrant echoes of myself.

Four fine lines
From left to right
Hosting rhythm and melody within the
Framework of inflexible flats and sharps,
Classically played is prepared and
Produced to be perfect—
The path so many traveled
And one has paved.

i am free jazz
no progression but the
spontaneous bursts of harmony I will
out of my hands with a delicate and
emotional force that can only exist
in a direct tunnel from the mind to the keys,
in a path only I myself have traveled and
in the path I myself have paved.

WALT WHITMAN HIGH SCHOOL
Joseph Pipolo

to walk the poet road
Sarah Sun

words are born from dead and swamped places. my room
has no windows, so i know when spring comes by the look
on my mother's face, like dragonflies out in the sun and
dreams stamped in gravity. at morning i have the urge
to shove the stiff bones of speeches down my throat
until my stomach bulges like an eye. to grin—my wide,
watermelon mouth—crinkling green skin. at noon, i am
so strong, i refuse to whisper in verse. my toes are
freezing, yet my heart is hot, catching a documental
black & white galaxy in the mirror. at the crux there are
soft spat-out sentences screen-snaking, but it is all just
paper. at evening, my murmurs are not heard, swallowed
by the ritual of some great, fiery beast, drumming
folklore through my skull. braided rivers trickle over
my forehead and pool on my lashes, like a red-browed
finch. at midnight, all at once, i am urgent. flushed
xanthic whites touch my pupils like tears. i am
inquietude. i blink like a songbird and the open road
blinks back. for what reason do the heavens bar me
from shoving my fist down my throat, thinly, to thieve
scores of couplets? for what quiet, garish glee do my
lettered torments dance? no. i am the great beast, taking
the whole world into my mouth. waning and waxing
like a real poet. it is morning—on my mother's face is
the soft kiss of sunlight, so in me there is
a small voice,
singing.

A women's "open road"
Alissa Olivera

Little girls dream of traveling the open road,

Women dream of traveling without the fear of passing by a man looking to unload.

Little girls smile at the strangers they encounter wondering if they'd like to see the world too,

Women only smile at the sunsets and mountains they've uncovered before the night sky turns blue.

An open road with kind strangers and beautiful sights is only a thing to imagine,

That is at least when you've been born with breasts in a world where man acts like there's a famine.
An open road to all is an open road to men,

And the little girls who have yet to discover the hunger in a young man's eyes once you turn ten.

Amusement parks and beaches holding the serenity you've always craved,

But that serenity can vanquish the minute you come into contact with someone who may see you and decide to be misbehaved.

The doubt, the fear, the uneasiness in your stomach will never be better on the open road.

The bumps and turns will only make it worse until either you or someone else decide to explode.

But in a perfect world the open roads are meant for all,

Girls and women alike enjoy the sunsets and late night drives without worrying about the danger that could befall.

We are not in a perfect world though,

We are on earth, where the darkness holds evil and a no is never a no,
Where little girls dream of traveling the open roads,
To soon wake up as women only safe in their closed off abodes.

Category E, Individual Poem Grades 11–12
NORTH BABYLON HIGH SCHOOL
Dr. Kaiser

Key or Gate
Aurelia Turano

The power a piece of paper can hold A
ticket, a train, a plane, a boat, a bus
A couple tickets can take me anywhere in
the world with a station, a landing site If you
pay the price, you get a key
A set path, a convenient Point A, Point B, But is
that really where I wish to be?
Looking out windows passing the world by
Seeing not stopping to see, just watching clouds pass Tickets
can only take me to a station, a landing site Two legs or a car
can take me everywhere, everywhere But walk through the
wrong forest
Along the wrong beach, drive too fast,
A gate imposed, from my Point A, Point B So
that is the choice, how to see the world
From station to station watching missed places
or wander everywhere, make a mistake and meet a gate,

What shall it be? A choice between Point A and B The
gate? Or the key?

WALT WHITMAN HIGH SCHOOL
Joseph Pipolo

Road Trip to 2014
Benjamin Wang

Seeking green-light independence,
I'll drive up highway 80,
heading to the Rocky Mountains.
Out the window
will be fields of yellow flowers,
bald eagles soaring over lakes,
Snake River's white rapids crashing,
herds of grazing bison flicking their tails,
and the snowy peaks of the Grand Tetons
coming into view. This time,
I'll stop to take pictures for Mom
of the panoramic blue.
As I drive along cliffs,
gusts will shake my car. "Don't worry,"
Dad's voice in my head will say,
and I'll feel safe again. I'll turn the knob on the radio,
searching for pop, but find only Dad's country.
I'll pull up to a rest stop and buy beef jerky,
coffee, and postcards to send home.
I'll drive down the road where
the cabin was, just a concrete slab now
that holds our blanket-fort and scary-movie memories.
I'll find a motel in that tiny town, next to
the closed-up cherry stand where we piled up pits,
our mouths stained red, next to the boarded-up movie theater,
where we watched dragons on the big screen,
next to the frozen pond, still scarred by ice skates.

The sky will grow so dark that I'll look for the Milky Way,
but find only Polaris, guiding me back home.

DOUGHERTY VALLEY HIGH SCHOOL
Lena Hymet

loose change
Elaina Li

loose change
look into my irises,
can you see the path that i've travelled?
the present's twists and turns? the future views?
do tinted windows spill the secrets of a soul? the inspirations? the successes? the failures?

cracked and twisted concrete, fear your mother's back
pennies, aged with patina, dropped, never to be picked up again
potholes filled with the sky's tears, streaked with regret
still, nevertheless, adorned with fading chalked art, never to be redrawn after the rain tides

rarely do i see the natural, the earth, the constellations, the romantic
often, however, i do walk hooded and disguised, on my own fogged sidewalks,
afraid of ghost hauntings, reminders of a better past
look into my eyes and tell me that it is worth distinguishing and not hiding

constant thoughts of what could be of my avenues
past drawn images haunt my realism, my pessimism
homey vibrant comfort hugging dressed sidewalks decorated with color and conversation,
turned to empty streets desecrated, eroded by icy expanses

never sufficient with small gratification or the ground stood upon
looking for a better something, even if just a fragment or flash
only thing never littered is my brain, not that i haven't tried,
like an obnoxious child, it never stops hoping and whining in its endless dissatisfaction

Buddhism in the Morning
Evan Wang

On the curbside, I utter
unprayers under my breath because
my mother once told me I was a child
pushed out by the grace of Buddha. The day
hasn't fathered me yet. This pale light, shadows
wantless on the sidewalk, never denting.
I see the roadwork not yet started, the edge
of the world so far ahead, shift and it'll shatter.
I shifted, and saw a squirrel's fleshed out corpse
splattered against asphalt. I was meant to see it. I do not
know why. Earlier, before I left the house
to come back, I stood between my closet and my bed,
trying this life on for size. When my quiet aunt
undressed herself, everyone gossiped about solitude,
dancing pasts, the buried blessing. I find it everywhere
I'm not supposed to be—in the dream where
I pushed my father away. Now, at the unforgiven
house, there are no family photos on the walls.
The second home a few blocks down, the birds falling
out of trees, the necklace hidden in a pencil case,
everything so stuck, so in its place.

9 and a half
Jeffrey Valle

The pebbles in the grooves
Share their space with the
violently pink gum
at the bottom of this size 9 and a half
Caked with the mud of last week
And covered in the dirt of today
Deteriorating soles and
Frayed laces
Form the frame of a shoe
That should be cast aside
But the comfort provided
By this size 9 and a half
Could never be replicated
By a size 10 that
Has not been to
the beach,
The forest,
the public restroom
The way this 9 and a half has

th(ink)
John Zsamboky

so, i know a road, a road of books

lined with covers, chapters, pages, paragraphs, sentences, words, letters, ink

the same ink i bleed onto the page when i write
the same ink that pours out of the pen like the words pour out of my heart
this road, the road less traveled, or at least as i see it

led me to you

because for a while i walked by myself
reading along this road and following a path that had been assigned to me
until i realized i could write my own path, take my own road

so i wrote myself a road, one unlike any other
because it was only mine, or at least i thought

until i met you

turns out you read along the same path the entire time
but my head was too far down to notice
and when i wrote my own road, i wrote you in it
even though i had no idea you existed

so i wrote with every bit of naive hope i failed to use as a child
that i would find you

and somehow it worked
by some miracle, what was once a thought, or a hope, is now so real

not real by accident or by luck
but real because our paths were meant to cross
and although it took me 17 years to look up

i finally saw you

and i instantly knew that you had been with me all along
even though i was too preoccupied to notice

there had to be someone on the same seemingly lonely road as me
with their head down looking for the answer to their prayers

and thank god we lifted our heads up to look
because now we travel the road together

CHAMINADE HIGH SCHOOL
Meaghan Dodson

Domesticated Poetry
Nuala Mernin

And I'm pulled in two directions
To the hall, the Bulging Brown
Beating
With a Bright Blue Broom
And the faded Beige print Of a crawl up the wall

Unhinge my ankles
Let me slam my Brain against the ceiling
'Till I Burst
'Till I fall
'Till I trickle down the wall

But I'm out, unfettered
But I'm pieces on the patio

And I drag my way to Brooklyn
Legs pulling arms, arms pulling face
But my Brain is stagnant, still
And I'm pulled in two directions

To the hall,
To the Burst of Brown Banging voices
To my Bloodstains on the wall

Walking to the free
To the Balanced meals
To the lovesick language of
Poets and surplus money

And it's down the ivory road
Where the air is cold and clean

There's no hall
No Boasting Beating Banging
Of my screams against the wall

And I'm pulled in two directions.

Destiny; Manifested
Olivia Robitsek

As the crystalline sheets of ice slowly faded, a brook of babbling scarlet sprouted from the infant earth.
Endless veins deep underground, fluid and magnetic;
A bewitching, wild road, where only the stars have a say.
The road was ripe and seductive.
She first flowered with dogwoods;
A solemn promise of life and liberty for the hopeful nomads that lavished in the glow of her affection.
Red roses and peach blossoms,
Mountain-laurel and evergreens blossomed in abundance along her coast.
Two great mountains guard the wild prairie where bison wade through golden Indiangrass.
She is hardly burdened by the blistering dust and the raw water that ceaselessly strikes her from the west.
Her children were cowboys and continentals who drifted fearlessly to hazy salvation with nothing but a melody and a folktale.
As shattered glass dotted the night sky of the old world next door, the road's lonely pearl was blitzed and blighted.
It was at that very moment that the inexhaustible rhythm of the road seemed to go silent.
From then on her blood was hemorrhaged into factories,
Fueling transistor radios and color T.V.s,
Musical synthesizers and the Chevy Corvette.
The open road had become the Great-Big-Cul-de-Sac.
Some lost their brothers in the old world next door,
They forgot the rhythm but not the melody.
They knew that they were still cowboys.
They knew that there was nowhere to go but everywhere;
And so they traipsed on under the stars that govern the road.
They soon learned that the pull of the road could not be belittled by the fat rays of sun that burned the nape of their necks or by the mechanical smog that deflowered their breath.
The golden road flows wherever stars still shine like passing ships;
She'll always be irresistible to all of us cowboys.
The road flowered her final forget-me-nots as close as she could to heaven;
For she knew that they would never be plucked.

CLASS ANTHOLOGY, GRADES 3 & 4

Category G

Grand Champion

Birch Pages - Writing Club
Ms. Lopez—Grade 4
BIRCH SCHOOL

New mood, New place
Sophia Gassi

Still in a mood
Needing time to breath
So I travel the open road.
The moon is so deep.
Right and wrong being strong
Open space.
Got to go to a new place
A new place,
A new road.
Now I know what it feels like to go.
Down and deep,
Seeing what it means.
Being strong,
So I don't do it wrong.
Round and round and round
To a new place
A strong person, IS a strong new place.
Value the time you have in that new place.
Every day is a new day.
New mood, New place.
The end

El Camino Abierto
Samantha Jimenez

No matter what struggles or challenges you are going through
Tu nunca vas esta sola
Por que estoy a tu lado
And when you are up
Or when you are down
Or when you are achieving your goals
Vamos a celebrar
I won't let a day of our friendship pass us.
Whenever you need a friend
I will be here for you.
All that we are that is sufficient
Our friendship will be strong forever
Des de a cuando tomó el camino abierto

People of the Open Road
Brynn J. Arnone

On the open road you will find many people,
some rude,
some kind,
it all depends on the people you find.
Sometimes you find creatures on the open road,
a slug,
a snail, a frog
or a toad.
So go,
go on to the open road
where you will find many people,
some rude,
some kind,
it all depends on the people you find.

Beauty Of The Open Road
Brynn J. Arnone

Officially the most beautiful place is the open road
Perfect beauty on the open road
Everything is beautiful on the open road
Not typical beauty much more on the open road

Really beautiful on the open road
Open roads are lively and beautiful
All the beauty is here on the open road
Definitely the most beautiful place is the open road

The Open Road
Quinn Dennehy

I am welcome to the open road
So many colors reflecting on the creek
Such magical day in the fall
Leaves are falling down
A nice picnic with a bunch of food
Let my imagination flow
So many colors Seeing rainbows and unicorn
See the beauty of the world Let the universe take control
It is a risk, a risk to take
Me having my own bubble
No rules
just me my rules
Me and my family
My sister is playing with me
My mom and sister
the ones that support me
Fancy dinner me wearing a dress
Going to a dance on the dance floor
Happiness inside me
No more stopping to think
My family supporting me the whole way
The open round
I am free finally

My family
Joshua

I carry them with me wherever I go
My dad very caring and very kind
My brother is daring with a very curious mind
My mom very courageous with outrageous love
My grandma is dramatic and very frantic
My grandpa loves me the most and its fantastic

The Amazing World We Are
Aiden Hunkler

I take the open road
Determined and persistent
An amazing, confident, and kind world beyond the horizon
All the encouragement that I have received
I can't give up unless it stops
But I know it will never stop
I am loved
I am happy
I show perseverance
My future is bright
I will succeed and I know that
I won't ever give up on my dreams
My dreams are my future
Dreams are goals that I will achieve
The beautiful land of joy
All the healthy people
That don't give up
They are proud
Even if it's cold
Hot
Warm
Or freezing
I will never give up on my dreams!
We are an amazing world

Beauty Of The Open Road
Eloise Brennan

Open road
No limits
No expansion
Run, run
No stopping
I am free for the first time
The smell of the flowers
The breeze in my hair
There's no hiding
There's just being me
There's no holding me back
There's no going back
No one is taking control of me
The universe above
The beauty of the world
Lies in the palm of my hand
I can go anywhere
I can see anything
No thinking about my stress
No thinking about my schoolwork
No one judging me
No parents No sisters
No friend that I have to talk to
Just me running
On the open road

Untitled
Kaley Mohan

Oh, the view on the open road
Practically a wonder
Endless world of imagination
Never disappoints me

Really pretty
Open road,
A beautiful place
A heaven when you're alive
Don't stress about the open road

Open road Poetry 2
Eloise Brennan

Am I dreaming Am I awake
Are my eyes closed Are they open What to do
What to say Doesn't matter On the open road I am here
All alone
I could be sad Happy
Angry Glad mad
I could be anything on the open road Don't have to think if I'm right or wrong Don't even have to think to go left or right Don't have to pretend
Don't have to worry Don't have to stop Not on the open road

The Amazing World We Are
Aiden Hunkler

I take the open road
Determined and persistent
An amazing, confident, and kind world beyond the horizon
All the encouragement that I have received
I can't give up unless it stops
But I know it will never stop
I am loved
I am happy
I show perseverance
My future is bright
I will succeed and I know that
I won't ever give up on my dreams
My dreams are my future
Dreams are goals that I will achieve
The beautiful land of joy
All the healthy people
That don't give up
They are proud
Even if it's cold
Hot
Warm
Or freezing
I will never give up on my dreams!
We are an amazing world

CLASS ANTHOLOGY, GRADES 7 & 8

Category I

Grand Champion

Our Journeys
Nicole Pomaro—Grade 8, Period 9
MOUNT SINAI MIDDLE SCHOOL

A Harmonious Sea
Malia A.

"Up on deck," "Up on deck," a term I've heard before,
From the many friends that I still have, and by those who were left on the bay.
We travel through the murky waters of hate and dark and storm
Just so we can have a future
    Of hugs and games and
                love.

Friendship is a way of life, a sea of salty swirls,
A sea that is not polluted, but still unclear, unclear as the destiny that lies before us.
I hear the sounds of laughing, even crying tears of joy.
The tears are the smell of the ocean waves.

But it's far away, oh so far away.
Friends may not be forever, but this journey will be.
The challenges that we may face may change our relationship forever
Our boat rocks with the doubt of our friendship and the changes that come with it.
The masts flap of the winds of the held breath of our companions, and the wooden poles creak with bitterness.
My sisters and brothers float on this boat with the strength of our bond. We ride these waters for a better friendship—another family.

Away on a Journey
James B.

Away on a journey I will go. I will go to many places.
I will do many things.
I will meet many people.
Away on a journey I will go.

I may go to the beautiful city Dublin in Ireland,
To the snowy, towering Tatras in Poland,
To the rolling landscape of the Black Forest of Germany,
To the massive Colosseum in Italy.
Away on a journey I will go.

A Future Beyond
Rilynn B.

I search this vast land, and I search for places unknown,
I meet and greet people from different lands.
I hope for these new opportunities, and I beg for a career.
Listen well, and heed the words of the wise.
Study, study, study, study is what will be on my mind at all times.
Work hard for the future beyond,
Take the leap of faith for the future beyond.
Encourage others to follow their hopes and dreams,

Tell those who will listen to work hard.
I seek a future where I will be with new people,
Where I will work harder than before.
I work hard so I have the freedom later in my journey,
For the future beyond.
My journey is just beginning.
Onward, to the future beyond.

The Grand Plan
Connor B.

Life is like a burrito: so many different components bound together into something
More grand.
I've yet to know all the layers of my life, or exactly where I'll go.
Maybe I'll go to the snowy tops of Kilimanjaro,
Or the inferno of Beirut.
Perhaps college and a career are the paths I'll take.,
But I'll stop to say "Hello" even if I'm heading towards Bordeaux.

I will see the silky smooth snow of Kilimanjaro, and the Monstrous Mountains of
  Beirut.
I will see the tremendous towers of the city where I will work.
I will see the curious college students traverse the cities.
I will see it all.

I will hear the raucous roar of the mountains,
I will hear the powerful people from each city I cruise.
I will hear them all.

I will overcome the rageful heat of Beirut.
I will overcome my subjective peers who hover over my work.
I will overcome the tremendous terror of my trade.
I will overcome it all.

I will learn that in times of pain, I must remain patient,
I will learn to neglect those subjective peers.
I will continue to remember that life is but a burrito:
Each part on its own is great, but together they are grand.

My Open Road
Autumn B.

My open road allows me to become a new person.
I leave the worries of the real world behind for just a moment.
My open road lies in airplanes guiding me through the cotton candy clouds to a whole new world,
Watching the pastel colors of blue and orange melt into the world below me while
I'm thousands of feet in the sky.
The excitement of seeing new faces places me on Cloud Nine.

As soon as I touch the ground, I feel the warm summer air on my skin.
I look up and see the stars shining like a thousand diamonds.
The exotic smells fill my senses.
The words people seem to just throw around are harder for me to pick up,
But this only further piques my curiosity.

Things are so unlike the things I am used to at home.
I feel like I have entered a whole new world.
Here, there are new things for me to learn and see.
I can see things I have never seen before.
I can gain new knowledge of a new way of life I didn't know existed before.
My open road is the whole world.rooted firmly beneath my feet.

Take Me Home
Rachael B.

The journey seems to never halt.
When will it be ending?
I've been through thick and thin,
I've seen strengths and flaws,
But where will I end up?

All the twists and all the turns,
I continue to return to the one place I call home.
My journey leads back,
Through fights and hugs,
Through the appetite of jealousy…
They all lead me back to you.

Yes, home may be a place, But not for all.
My home could be here or there, or anywhere…
As long as I'm with you.
I feel your warmth while you hold me here, and I know I've ended my journey.
My road could be never-ending.
I wouldn't mind as long as you were by my side.

My best friend,
Through the bests and the worsts,
You never fail to make me smile.
I may not have started the journey with you,
And there have been cracks in my road,
But I know that wherever I go,
I will always find my home in you.

My Highway to High School
Zahara C.

My route to high school is simple.
I want to seize the opportunities cast my way,
And be able to succeed in the long run.

My route to high school is simple.
I hope to have fun in my classes,
But also get valid grades.

My route to high school is simple.
I hope to enjoy my adolescent years,
But also experience my youthful adult era.

My route to high school is simple.
I hope to make new friends,
And to generate new memories.

My route to high school is simple.
I hope to graduate someday,
And prove to myself that I not only did it,
I paved my own highway to success.

Voices
Leah C.

Rising once more,
After a remarkable journey.
A journey that was cherished throughout time,
And will continue to last eternally.
Once nothing more than an object,
Now an old friend.
Chatters of a vibrant concert hall begin to diminish as I step forward.
Lifting up my violin in the midst of the stillness,
Resting my chin, just as I did years ago.

As the smooth hairs are placed on the coarse metallic strings,
A deep breath is taken.
The hall is silent, but my mind is occupied.
Drawing back the bow, the violin lets out a sonorous tone,
An eager voice to take on the world,
Filling the room with euphoria and amusement. The
tension in my body relaxes as I continue to play,
With the bow gliding across the string like a ship on the water.

As the strings cry out vibrantly,
I hear the voices of my father and my instructor,
The same voices that guided me through my journey.
The voices that taught me to persevere and overcome obstacles in life.

My Dream
Francesco D.

To be so sure of where I want to be,
But not what I dread facing on the way,
This is the dream that I imagine.

That at any moment, I could be at the beach
The salty smell of the ocean in my nose,
My feet, buried in the hot sand, with a cold drink in my hand,
The sound of waves crashing down on the shoreline,
And the big blue sky above me, watching and admiring from above.

At that moment, I will have made my dream a reality,
And at only that moment,
I can rest easily.

I would look back and recall who had helped
And who has faulted.
I would acknowledge them
Like my closest friends and family.

Then I would think about life beyond this one,
Among the fallen ones.
That is my dream.

Carpe Diem
Giorgia G.

To make the most of the present time and give little thought to the future...
Wherever I end up is where my decisions take me
Whoever I end up with is whoever decides to follow.
Thinking about where I will be in the future takes away from the now.
Knowing this, would I continue to plan ahead?
Whatever it is I want to do, I shall do it now,
In fear of fantasizing too far in time.
To use time wisely is something that needs to be understood.
Not knowing where I will be,
What I will see, smell, hear, taste, or touch is a daunting concept.
Despite this, would I still forget the future?
The answer is whatever I make of it.
"Carpe Diem" is an urge.
Just an urge, but an urge that can depict what the future holds.
Seize the day, as one would say,
But I wouldn't entirely disregard what the future carries.
The future is a long way away, and my road is yet to be finished.
If one was to remember,
Carpe Diem.
To make the most of the present time and give little thought to the future.

White House
Nathanael H.

As I speak on the paramount podium
In front of a colossal crowd of people,
I shout words of inspiration and prosperity
Into a white house pridefully.

My feet rest on a righteous red rug,
While I am seated on a regal chair. With
a pen in hand I have robust power, And
with it comes robust responsibility.

As the pen strokes the document,
America becomes illuminated by freedom and justice.
And when I walk out my office,
All of America will be there cheering together.

Later I will enter bed,
Knowing that I accomplished something great.
I will fall asleep as peaceful as a dove
And wake up as stressed as a gazelle being chased.

I turn television channels,
Seeing slander and disgust toward me.
I will wonder what I've done wrong,
And realize this job is wrong.

I can't make everyone happy,
I can't make people come together,
I can't make wrong seem right,
What does wrong and right even mean?

An impossible job is what I've chosen,
A job only for madmen and saints.
I walked an open road of freedom,
But with freedom comes just as many treacherous roads as it does glorious ones.

Some Walks You Take Alone
Sophia H.

Every road can be open.
Some people do not see it that way.

Sometimes roads are worn down and no longer visible,
But they're still there.
Sometimes roads have different pathways and different opportunities.
But there can always be more than one right path.
Sometimes there are obstacles that interfere with your road.
But there is always a way to overcome an obstacle.

I don't know where my road will lead.
But I pledge to be happy, with where it ends.
Everyone should be.

Always, I will travel with curiosity.
Always, I will remember my reward, whatever it is.
Always, I will acknowledge that the hardships I meet will bring me strength.

I will see the goodness of the road.
I will hear all the glorious things on the road.
I will meet new customs and cultures.
I will reach my destination.

Sunny Graduate
Emily H.

After taking the highway to high school,
I'll want to go back to before.
Kindergarten was joyful, and high school will feel like a war.
At the end, proud parents and friends will sit in the crowd.
The bright smiles of many,
Applause and whistles loud.
Everyone will watch as I stand with a diploma in hand,
The flashing of the camera as it goes click.
The principal will congratulate me, and off the stage I go quick.
I'll step on the last stair,
Realizing I'm no longer there.
And after I'm off that stage I'll go back never.
It's gone, I'm free, but the memories stay with me forever
-From crayons to pens,
And children's stories to textbooks. As I get older,
Things change but I know I'll journey far.

Truthful Future
Charlotte L.

The place of pure paradise is where I long to be.
The place of brotherhood to all who enter, with glowing faces and astonished smiles.
Where everyone recognizes everyone. Where happiness thrives, and never dies. This place of dreams, I hope to reach, but I have doubts I will at times.
"Am I good enough?" I often ask myself. "How do I know for sure?"
Sometimes I wonder if it is even real at all. What if I spend my whole life longing for a paradise that doesn't even exist?

Although I ask myself these questions, I know deep down I believe it does.
Heaven. It is described as a magical place. There, everything is according to God's Will. Everything is bright and full of joy.
Purgatory, I think, is the space in between. Between Hell, Earth, and Heaven.
It is the place your soul travels to before entering Heaven.
I imagine it to be a large white room, filled with people, all waiting for the same destiny in paradise.
I don't know how long I'll be waiting there, no one does. I wonder if time even exists there. If it does, I hope I won't have to wait long.

I find myself questioning my future a lot.
I worry about the bad outcomes, all of the decisions I must make, and how they can completely change my life.
Change is scary. It's often why I question things—thinking about the outcomes of my actions. When things are going well, I feel there is no need for change.
But truly, I believe that God is going to change things for our sake. He doesn't want us to suffer,
But sometimes we must, maybe to learn a lesson or change our mindsets.
There is a life ahead of me, one I might not be ready for, one I may never see or expect to come.
But I will keep moving forward and trust that God will bring me where I need to be.

Journey to Find Myself
Ryan L.

The need for peace and silence takes me away.
The journey there seems long, and the end almost unreachable. The
tense, constant chatter has me not wanting to stay where I am. The
longing for peace and silence fills my head.

I hear the little chirps of the birds, feel one with nature and one with myself.
I can taste the fresh air and feel like the people mentioned in books I've read.
The birds are a beautiful sight to see as they soar through the sky, carefree.
The forest is so large, I don't know where to go, but the destination doesn't matter.
It's the journey that fills me with glee.

As I walk through the forest, I am confronted by an obstacle - a downed tree blocks my path.
There is no way around it, so I must climb it.
One step at a time, until I reach the top.

There are no words to describe what I see.
I've finally learned that this world is a beautiful place.

Blast Off!
Anna M.

All my life has been training, training for this very moment.
I will blast off and take a journey into the unknown; a place where nobody has ventured.
I am in my seat, grasping for safety.
I hope not to move on, but to look ahead.
Three,
Two,
One.
I can't hear a thing; I feel immense pressure keeping me down.

When I finally can, I look back to the planet of my past life -My
family, my friends, and everything that I have ever known.
I am headed to a place new and adventurous, a place where I can make a change.
I feel my adrenaline kicking in, and I scream.
I am alone.
I feel excited.
My thoughts are everywhere. They keep slipping away from my head.
And then it hits, an impact big enough to break your bones.

When I open my eyes, I see that I have landed. I see a place waiting to be sculpted into something beautiful.
My life has taken me to a place with nothing, a place that I need to make my own.
A new life that I can create, doing whatever I want to do.

I step onto the ground, and it feels like clouds under my feet. It smells of fresh new air,
I hear the wind whistling, and I can't imagine a better place to be.

Path to Peace
Daniel M.

My road seems never-ending.
As far as I can see, God will never shine his luck down on me.
There are many obstacles., However, as far as I can see,
Music leads my path to peace.

As I leave middle school and high school, my viola in hand,
I smell and feel that fresh summer breeze,
And finally begin to understand how
I shall continue my path to peace.

Later on, I see myself playing my heart out in Carnegie Hall,
And a loved one watching as I do.
As my orchestra finishes its piece, I decide to walk further down my road.
And to my very own surprise, there are few people on my path to peace.

I see my mother and father, supporting me the whole way.
I see my siblings, showing affection when needed.
I see the embodiment of anxiety, running away from me.
As the road comes to an end, I think I fully understand my path to peace.

I learned much on my road, much about music and affection.
I've chased away anxiety and other fears.
And most importantly, I discovered that
Music leads my path to peace.

Freedom
Madeline P.

Salty air.
Gentle winds singing through the afternoon.
Afternoon heat roasting the sand below me,
That meets the angry ocean before me.
And in the ocean, a large ship,
Chained, awaiting freedom.

Freedom calls me.

Louder and louder,
The temptation grows.
My steps grow into sprints toward something I have longed for.
An adventure.
Full of surprises,
Full of laughter,
Full of cries
Of not knowing.

Not knowing the world that I get to stand on,
Except that it is something great,
Something great that must be seen.

I will not come back until I am satisfied.

The Road to the Afterlife
Nicholas P.

I wake up on the warm side of my bed and I feel better than usual,
Like I'm being lifted.
The warm hands on my back, pulling me up, feels better than anything I've ever felt.

I can't speak or move. I'm just there.
Soon I start to see things of my past, I
see a hospital, the one I was born in.
The hand places me in a room.

I see my mom holding a baby...me.
Then the warm, merciful hand picks me up. We glide through my childhood and then make another stop.
Here is when I met my best friend, one of the most meaningful moments of my life.
He was everything to me.

On to a football field during my senior year when I broke the touchdown record for my school.
That banner still means everything to me.
When I'm feeling down, I just go look at it, and it makes me feel better knowing I've done something.

On to Indianapolis, where I was drafted.
This is my most-proud moment ever, everything I've worked for paying off.
Then to an arcade, where I brought my wife on our first date.
We are young and joyful. She's my everything, and losing her would wreck me.
She's the reason I keep on pushing.

We're back at the hospital, but this time it's a mini-me being born.
My dream has come true.
Then the clouds get dark, and the hand stops at a funeral home.
I remember one of the biggest setbacks I've ever faced. I loved them so much.

Suddenly, I fall. Everyone I love walks by waving, saying I love you.
A bright light blinds me, and I feel warm.

Clear Waters
Saige R.

I will take my journey somewhere far away,
Not to the mountains, not to the lake.
Somewhere where the smell of salt is so strong, I think I can taste it.
Somewhere I can feel sand beneath my feet.

My journey will take me to the clear ocean,
With a light blue tint, quite like the sky,
With waves, alive and crashing,
And the wind whistling a song I think I've heard before.

Maybe my journey will take me to the islands of Hawaii,
Or maybe to the beaches of Turks and Caicos.
Maybe my journey will take me to the Amalfi Coast of Italy,
Or maybe to the clear waters of Jamaica.

Regardless of where I go,
I know I will make my home by clear waters.

Journey Through School
Jordan S.

Still young and inexperienced, I embark on a journey.
Hard work, troubles, and friendships await.
The long, smelly, and curved halls lead me to my next destination.
I make it through the day after many hardships, only to return the next.
This road is one of many episodes.
My friends and family will guide me through my journey.
Information will flow through my brain like a waterfall.
I will learn to harness this information and make use of it.
I will overcome the endless tests with this knowledge.
I will make many mistakes, but I will use them as a way to improve.
I hope the many tedious and extensive trials will end in my favor.
I hope the flames of youth still run through me as I mature.
My road will lead me to become more independent and developed.
By the end of my journey, I hope to be filled with knowledge like the ocean is filled with water.
When the journey is over, the hard work will all be worth it.

Long Drive
Noah S.

Driving through the snowy hills,
Rocks and streams around the path I travel.
Starving, I grab a bite to eat and set out on the highway.
There is a glare from traffic lights on my face as I drift off to sleep,
Only to be woken up by a bump in the road.
I look off to the side to see beautiful snowy trees and large rocks.
The wind is blowing rapidly on my face and my hair is swaying back and forth.
Beggars are on the side of the roads.
There is silence except for the sound of the breeze.

I continue traveling, wondering how close our destination is.
It feels as if we had not moved from our start, and that we would never get there.
I recognize the store fronts as we approach our destination.
I can already smell the aroma coming from my grandparents' house,
Only a few more turns and I would arrive in Canada.

Journey Through Teenage Years
Lylah S.

Though it won't be easy I can say,
We will wish we could go back to those good old days.
We will wish to be young and naive,
We will wish we were still happy and free.

The laughter and cries,
Sorrys and goodbyes,
This is all part of the journey through your teenage years.
For me, there will be no wasting my days knowing I will never be getting them back.

I will build friendships that last a lifetime.
I will grow older, looking back on good memories with these friends,
The friends who cared for me and loved me for who I am.
I will look back on the happiest times of my life and be grateful.

The road I walk down will be like a surprise,
Not knowing what comes next, I will
Just live life,
With no regrets,
Having fun,
Because soon these good old days will end,
And my teenage days will become memories.

The Small Things
Liana W.

Up the hill of hardship,
Where the moon of success shines,
With friends and family coming along,
Everyone is here.
Going and going through school,
And finally reaching,
The end of it all.

It's the final few years of this hill of hardship,
Friends come with it,
And the musty, sweet smell of books.
After years and years, we have finally done it.
We have completed our schooling.
Our fate is now in our own hands,
As we leave the years behind,
The spacious hallways echo as we leave.

After the years have gone by,
We're in the world, prospering.
We learn a lesson that we've hadn't yet:
We must not strain ourselves to the limit.
We should find happiness with life,
In the small things like the crickets chirping,
And the birds flying.
We should examine the world closer,
And just live.

The Beach
Kailie W.

I take a walk along the beach,
Where the road never ends,
And the journey keeps going.
It's continuous.
Who knows when it will end.
The beach is calm, and there's no pressure to finish.
I can take my time and enjoy the journey.

The dolphins jump and splash freely.
Turtles crawl up and down the sand and into and out of the water.
They are safe.
They are free.
They are relaxed.

I can feel the warmth of the air with a cool ocean breeze passing through.
I hear the strong, loud, deep blue waves crashing,
It's as if the waves are telling a story.
I can feel the warm sand grains between my bare toes.
    I taste the cool vanilla ice cream melting in my
                                          mouth.
With each bite, a new feeling of chill flows through my body.

I see the clear blue skies with the sun shining down; there is not a cloud in the sky.
The journey goes on.
With each bite, each step, and each breath,
The journey continues.
My road goes on, and who knows when and where it will end.

 # Honorable Mentions

Sailing Spartans
A Collection of Off-Beat Journeys
Dr. Karl O'Leary Grade 8, Period 6

SODUS CENTRAL SCHOOL DISTRICT

Morgan Eastley
Dylan Robinson
Wade DeRue
Gabriela Miranda
Aguilera Murillo
Jacob Quinn
Ariana Montemorano

Ilysa Ziervogel
Brendan Harper
Daphne Creason
Simon Thomas
Xavier Baitsholts
Kyiah Wiley
Alex Selvage

Eduardo Sierra
Theo Grady
Izabelle Lamark
Lennon Zabelny
Thomas Curran
Karla Trejo

Where the Road Ends
Kelly Doran Grade 7 Period 3

MOUNT SINAI MIDDLE SCHOOL

Alejandro Acosta
David Bilski
Luke Buckhout
Alia Esen
Bradley Hirst
Jonathan Lavin
Jayden Mascaro
Jacob Mizzrahi
Aubrey Sigault
Joel Vasquez

Olivia Albertina
Sophia Bisceglie
Angelina DeVito
Justin Ferdinand
Dylan Izzo
Michael Llerena
Connor McLaughlin
Haley Nordstrom
Jacob Szczepanik

Fernando Arichabala
Emma Brock
Jaxson Dunne
Cole Hanauer
Gabriel Knoell
Makayla Marano
Alexander Miron
Ryan Pearl
Eva Urbinati

The Door to Dreams
Kelly Doran Grade 7 Period 7

MOUNT SINAI MIDDLE SCHOOL

Aiden Alessi	Andrew Anzaldi	Aiden Brower
Evangeline Carmody	Faith Chouloute	Alyssa Erdmann
Connor Fabin	Lainie Friedman	Drake Haas
Molly Hegreness	Gary Kaible	Omar Khan
Jack Lipari	Anna Mueller	Jaden Mui
Sienna Oldis	Chase Oppenheim	John Regazzi
Madison Reinhardt	Asher Sabia	Kieran Smith
Even Target	Victoria Taveras	

Away We go
Nicole Pomero Grade 8 Period 4

MOUNT SINAI MIDDLE SCHOOL

James A.	Natalie B.	Kevin C.	Rey D.
Mikayla F.	Eleanor H.	Kylie H.	Christian L.
Abbie L.	Karlie M.	Ella-Marie M.	Isabella P.
Sara P.	Peter R.	Leah S.	Zaina S.
Amiyah S.	Jenna S.	Braden V.	

Encounters on Life's Road
Nicole Wallace Grade 8 Period 6

MOUNT SINAI MIDDLE SCHOOL

Jenna S.	Hannah Bronleben	Collin Bruder
Andrew Cardone	James Casino	Bella Chen
Elly Chen	Laila Delaney	Connor Enxuto
Brodie Gargiulo	Jason Hayes	Gavin Hertz
Leah Kassebaum	Kirill Kayran	Madison Kelly
Courtney Lambert	Kylie Lehmann	Akira Lo
Dylan Madigan	Dante Maola	Luca Maola
Miavanessa Milicia	Genevieve Miller	Aarav Penagaluru
Sofia Perez	Leah Robert	Gabriela Santos
Aahna Soral	Alexa Surdi	Haley Wesnofske
Lily Zick		

Category I, Class Anthology Grades 7–8

CLASS ANTHOLOGY, GRADES 9 & 10

Category J

 Grand Champion

Alliance poétique!
Clare Chotiner—Grades 9-10
HICKSVILLE HIGH SCHOOL

Waltz of Tomorrow
Aanya Rawal

A child, silent specter on the road I once tread,
Her presence, a mirror echoing the words left unsaid,
Beckoning in a language both known and strange,
    "je suis là,"[1] said she,
Familiarity entwined with the voice of change.

In my gaze, lingers the essence of "Je ne sais pas qui je suis,"[2]
Whispers of a past, etched forever,
Each step, a ballet of lost memories and dreams, on this path was where reality gleamed.

Les moments précieux, like jewels on the ground, I picked up, marked the road as mine, le chemin,[3]
Tiny moments, comme secrets, the road holds
Paroles d'amour, whispered by the breeze,

A symphony of languages that the girl could read
The road, un tableau d'émotions et de désirs,[4]
Painted with strokes of passion, anger and despair
    Chaque pas [5], une danse with the shadows of time,
A tapestry woven with nostalgia
Whispers of tomorrow, mingling with the past,

So, on the road I tread, with the silent child,
La route, un poème in the language of the heart
Where the Girl converses, transcending moi

1 "I am here"
2 " I do not know who I am"
3 "The path"
4 "A table of emotion and desires"

Journey of the soul
Nandini Bali

As the roads to my soul uncovers, a journey unfolds,
From the innocence in life to wisdom and bold.
The questions arising where will I go? Whom will I see?
Having me think deep into me.

In the crowd of thousands, I'll wander far and wide,
Gliding through highs and lows to find the desired pride.
From the playgrounds of childhood to halls of learning,
It has been a path that has no ending.

As a child, I danced along the fields with my little small dream,
An unseen realm of a doctor's dream.
With every passing single day, the obstacles may arise,
Challenges to test my patience and my spirits to touch the skies.

Yet, along the way, some helpers I'll find,
Leading me through the dark, they'll remind.
Mentors and friends, their wisdom, they'll impart,
Nurturing the flame within, which ignites hope in my heart.

Through highs and lows, I'll learn and grow,
From the innocence in life to the doctor I'll know.
I'll heal, I'll fix, I'll comfort and care,
A lamp of ignited fire, spreading light everywhere.

d'amour et de mensonges
Sumaiya Barez

dans la voiture je vais, je roule
partout où le vent m'emmène, j'ai raison?
la vie devant moi clignote
avant de mourir, je vis
à mon maximum, je vois le monde des mensonges
les yeux qui mentent malgré la vérité
l'amour n'était qu'un mythe
pour moi de croire à ce destin
J'ai donné la cinquième chance de changer
le mensonge d' un adolescent garçon
n'a fait que tuer la joie
oh comme je regarde le monde différemment
Fini de montrer de la sympathie
j'essaie de rester fort mais ça prend trop de temps
peu importe, c'est la vie, je ne peux pas nier

The Voyage
Nicole Machowski

I look at the road.

Busy and loud.

I don't know what to do.

It's crowded and it can't get through.

Maybe I'll take another way.

It's harder but it'll be worth it.

Sometimes it is better to do something harder than easier, the result will be more exciting to receive.

I get to the other side, it's beautiful.

I needed to see this.

So I would know, the trip is more important than what's at your destination.

in the Spanish streets
Gabriel Martinez

In the Spanish streets, a boy was lost.

He was French and missed his mom
Oh how he thought of his old town
He appeared to only be a clown in a downtown

But as time went on it grew to him
He felt less and less grim
And although he missed his family
He found a world that was viewed so glamorously

It been a few months since he left
And with his class, he left his mother bereft
But soon enough he boarded the flight back to Paris
And the look on his mother's face was filled with bliss

Mère patrie!
Saadhvi Prasad

Came to our house, a tiny fairy.
Smiling, happy, cheerful and laughing.
Brightening our house with her small steps,
She resides in our hearts as a symbol of love.
She is the definition of 'amour',
As a mother and a sister.
She worries for others,
Her love for everyone shines brighter than the sun.
Enduring all the pain for herself,
She is the very joy that resides within,

Never refuses for anything,
Such love is no-one but our mother.
Supporting us through thick and thin,
Yet, we shred her to her skin.
In French she is 'mère patrie' and in English she is our motherland.
Every name describes her.
If we love her,
Then, why hurt her?
She is the strength of every bond there is.
No one can repay her debt
Because until I return home,
The prayer goes to her.
She is the embodiment of the world,
She is known as the great Mother earth.

Death sits
Shelby Fraser

Death sits in my living room
Turning the pages of a novel
Once read a decade before.

Death stands in the cold hallway
Hands offering a warm blanket
Sat in a closet I no longer open.

Death butters a piece of toast
Lounging at the table
In a chair left empty.

Death leaves my home at daybreak
When the mourning doves call And the wind whistles.

Death returns in the evening
Embracing me in a hug
That I have grown to accept.

New York Girl
Sruthi Nanugonda

At the time of her youth, a girl of fifteen years,

Her heart is a passion for the joys that nature brings.
She dances 'neath the sun, away from fears,
Outside her sanctuary, she spreads her wings.

With a love for pink, she paints her world bright,
In hues of passion, her spirit takes flight.
Cheering for the Yankees with all her might,
Their victories ignite her heart's pure light.

Oh, pizza divine, a culinary art,
A slice of heaven that captures my heart.
With cheese, sauce, and toppings so grand,
In each bite, pure bliss, forever I stand.

A traveler she is, eager to explore,
New lands, new cultures, an endless allure.
Decorating her dreams, a space to adore,
Organizing life's puzzle, solutions pure.

This New York girl, at fifteen years old,
A tapestry of passions, a story to be told.
Family, nature and the sun, her heart's gold,
A life of adventure, her dreams forever unfold.

Roaming the Unknown
Natasha Neira

I wandered through the open road,
Not knowing which way to go,
But knowing it's where freedom flows.
Wandering along in search of truth and grace,
I seek adventure to find my place.

The road, a path still so unknown,
Where dreams and creativity freely roam.
With every step, a new story unfolds.
A road I will continue to walk, till I grow old.

Through busy cities and tranquil towns,
I hear stories, I will soon disclose.
With each encounter, a lesson is learned
Yet, there is still so much to learn.

I stumble through the open road,
Still deciding which way to turn.
Many opportunities await in each and every turn.
I wander aimlessly, to seek my dreams,
Hoping to find peace in every seem.

So I journey on, with my head held high
Hoping to find answers beneath the sky.
Even though, I'm not sure where to go,
I'm sure the road will guide me to where I'm destined to go.

Nature
Anishka Dass

In forest deep, shadows sway,
Nature's dance, both night and day.
Whispers of wind, leaves they play,
Life's song echoing, come what may.

Mountains high, touch the sky,
Streams flow gently, as time flies by.
Fields of green, flowers bloom,
Nature's beauty, banishing gloom.

Sunrise, promise of the day,
Sunsets glow, nature's display.
In every leaf. In every tree,
Nature's wonders, for all to see

La nuit étoilée
Gerthaidjene Dufresne

Dans le silence de la nuit étoilée,
J'ai marché seul sur la plage déserte,
Le vent caressant mon visage fatigué,
Et les vagues chantant une mélodie offerte.

Les pas dans le sable ont marqué ma route,
Révélant une quête profonde et mystérieuse,
Cherchant des réponses au creux de ma voûte,
Laissant derrière moi une vie anxieuse.

L'océan m'a murmuré ses secrets anciens,
Me rappelant que la vie est éphémère,
Que chaque instant compte, qu'il n'est pas vain,
Et qu'il faut savourer chaque lueur éclairée.

Cette expérience m'a enseigné une leçon précieuse,
Que la solitude n'est pas synonyme de tristesse,
Qu'en soi réside une force enivrante et joyeuse,
Et que la vie offre des moments de tendresse.

Marcher seul sur cette plage a été un cadeau,
Une rencontre avec mon âme et mes pensées,
Dans cette expérience, j'ai trouvé mon flambeau,
Pour éclairer ma route et vivre en toute sérénité.

A lily just sprout
Angad Ahuja

A Lily is nothing like a rose they say.
It has no thorn to stain her beautiful way.
Same for the girl I write.
She is like a dove at any sight.
A dove as graceful can be.
And love is just what you see.
Sometimes it's all you think about.
Just like the Lily that just sprout.
The beautiful blue eyes.
Just like the color that fills the skies.
Her eyes remind me of the ocean.
It can squash a bug in one motion.
So in the end I can say.
She has not been left stray.
Lilies wilt
A thorn can be a sin.
It can leave a cut on your chin.
Your chin, your hand, your eye.
Where it leaves you left to cry.
I am but a bug.
Who is in need of a drug.
A drug to calm my mind.
In love I was blind.
The damage I gained.
My body is left stained.
Stained by a thorn.
It was a lily's horn.
Lily's can wilt.
They can leave you behind with guilt.
So now I've proposed.
Lilies are a drug I unclosed.

Dazed and Eager
Zabdi Amaya

Dazed and Eager,I step onto the open road

Where should the constellations take me on this road? The path is enlightened with the stars' luminosity

The Alicanto colors The Pitch black Night while Singing Its Ethereal Tune The Alicanto Colors my path While decorating the sky with Burning Stars The Alicanto Emits a bright Light to my path showing me my good fortune Entranced and Eager, I walk upon the road

Whirlwinds fill the night sky and The Alicanto Screeches

The stars fall one by one, one by one, No longer illuminating my path

The Stars Fall Into the Pitch Black Darkness, No Longer Leading me To My fortune The Stars Fall Onto My skin Burning and Aching as they Hit

Upon The Dark Road, I am Still Here Burning and Aching Unable to Move As I look down The Stars Are Etched Into my Skin

As I pass my finger, They start glowing, One by one, one by one

The Stars Have Become Part of my soul, Enlightening it making it full of purity

I am the light to my own path

My being illuminates the dark path as I start walking

My feet step onto shatters of stars wounding the soles of my feet

Shatters Of Stars Like Shatters Of Dreams Of Those That Couldn't Reach Them

The Alicanto returns for the light of its dear starlets I continue to walk the star broken path

I hear The Ethereal Song Of The Alicanto Once again

I hear The Ethereal Song Of The Alicanto In the Dark Distance Far away from me

I take a step and I take another, My Skin being the Only thing Illuminating My Path I am The Light to My Own Path

Dans le jardin de mon coeur
Gerthaidjene Dufresne

Dans le jardin de mon cœur fleurit un amour,
Un sentiment si doux, si pur et si sincère,
Les mots ne peuvent exprimer tout leur pouvoir,
Ils dansent sur les pages pour te les offrir.

Tes yeux brillent comme des étoiles dans le ciel,
Illuminant ma vie de leur éclat divin,
Chaque regard éveille en moi un feu éternel,
Et je me perds dans l'océan de ton regard malin.

Ta voix est une symphonie qui enivre mes sens,
Un doux murmure qui berce mon âme éprise,
Chaque mot est une caresse, une délicatesse,
Qui fait battre mon cœur et chavirer ma raison.

Ton sourire est un rayon de soleil dans ma vie,
Il dissipe les nuages de mes soucis et mes peines,
Il m'apporte la joie, la chaleur et l'envie,
Et dans ses courbes, je trouve la paix sereine.

À tes côtés, je me sens fort et en sécurité,
Tu es ma muse, mon inspiration sans fin,
Dans tes bras, je trouve l'éternelle félicité,
Et je sais que mon amour pour toi ne connaîtra jamais de fin.

Ce poème d'amour est dédié à toi, mon cher amour,
Pour te rappeler combien tu es précieux pour moi,
Chaque mot, chaque ligne, chaque vers est un tambour,
Qui résonne de notre amour, qui ne s'éteindra jamais, je le crois.

Dear traveler
Katerina Fragopoulos

Dear traveler,
Your words, your lines, your stanzas, are very moving.
You wish to travel. You wish to journey.
You wish to be unrecognizable in the crowd.
Your thoughts and plans are grand.

But here lies a problem;
You talk about escaping indoor complaints.
You talk about stepping outside of libraries.
You talk about the unwritten letters and the blank papers...

But here lies a problem;
You've just created another poem.
You've just created more pages that will be in a book.
This book will be in a library.
The poem in this book will be read by somebody.
The library will continue to exist because of poems like yours.

So, in summary, your poem while it was written very well
And took us on this journey where poems and books are forgotten.
Forgotten and replaced by paved roads, dirt roads, people we meet and the stars...
This poem has kept you from traveling because you took the time to write it.

And it's kept me from traveling because I took the time to read.

The boundless sky
Teresa Karmel

Upon the boundless sky, I gaze;
Its existence propels me into a delightful haze.
No confines nor shackles to endure,
The simplicity of this vast freedom itself never fails to stagger me.
Numerous distinct paths diverge ahead,
Maybe even teetering on the brink of inundation.
As countless inconsequential thoughts circulate in my mind,
I managed to conjure many queries that never before had been explored within my consciousness.
Perhaps it is the awareness of the nothingness that surrounds me that has caused such thoughts.
Whatever it may be, the feeling is most definitely incomparable.

Daisies
Khushleen Kaur

Daisies.
I wish I bloomed,
Like a daisy in the rain
Because daisies are my favorite.
But instead I'm covered in scars that I used to
Hide the pain.
I wish I was as open,
As a daisy in bloom,
Because I would be able to show myself
What hides in the corners of the worlds paths
The rest of the space being occupied,
By my pain.
I wish the daisies were bright
Like a pathway in the summer
Because I could finally find a new way
But too bad I opt to stay inside where no one
would ever reside.
But like a daisy in the autumn
Of course I will fall
My petals leaving my side
A dull, green color will cover me full
Now blending in with the crowd
What chances do I have now that I have been
Denied.

Ode to Whitman
Harshal Mehta

Afoot and light-hearted, I embark,
On the open road, the long path's spark,
Earth sufficient, stars in the dark,
Carrying tales, burdens old and hark.

Efflux of the soul, happiness profound,
Fluid character, joy in the sound,
Effusion of strength, on open ground,
Journeying together, in love unbound.

Allons! with power, elements untamed,
Sailing wild seas, where dreams are named,
Away from formules, where souls are famed,
Companions grand, in the universe framed.

To undergo much, tramps of days,
Fruition leads to greater maze,
Call of battle, turbulent ways,
Struggling forward through life's displays.

Camerado, give your hand,
Love more precious than gold, unplanned,
Stick together, bold, withstand,
On the road, a timeless strand.

Back home beneath the sky
Alayna Saqlain

Beneath the sky so vast and blue,

Lay an open road, cheerfully welcoming me.

A new journey unfolds, with whomever I please.

The scent of freedom fills the sweet air,

Not a care in the world as I navigate through.

The birds are chirping their sweet melody to me,

As a ray of sunlight eagerly paints the beautiful landscape.

I am overwhelmed with happiness and a sense of familiarity.

For every time I feel lost within myself,

I'll close my eyes and remember the open road, and know I'll always find my way back home.

The Ocean
Jennifer Arias Martinez

The water, sweeping in patterns and rhythm, surrounding me where I stand

The cold air breeze is soothing at night, while the sound of the waves are moving aimlessly

The sky and water so dark, yet so pretty and blue

The sand so soft and warm during the summer, it's so beige and pure

The light moon makes the water shine, whilst the airy clouds roam around carelessly without a care in the world

9
Mujhda Azimi

Even though I may not know who you are, traveling with you made me realize what we are.

The earth appears cruel and unknown, the animals seem cruel and unknown.
As you say, everything is rude and incomprehensible, I know how beautiful things could be beyond the use of words.

Once you get to know the world we live in, you see the true beauty it has as when you first viewed it.
Everyone must go and that we must understand, but everyone must understand the world before they go.

The creative stores, the beautiful buildings and the interesting inventions, they all remain but we do not.
We aren't meant to stay here forever but the kindness stays forever.

3 Haikyuu
Allison Chun

Open road awaits
Footsteps light, heart unburdened,
Life's path unwinds

The Path is tricky
Decisions to make now
Life's tale unfolds

Path to life's unknown
Journey's steps, each a lesson
Destiny awaits

The Open Road
Ramneet Kaur

The open road I see,
The wind is howling loud
That I can't hear my thoughts.
It's dark. There's no one here.

The further I go,
The darker it gets.
I listen, I try to hear.
But I only hear the wind.
What shall I do?
I look, I look for any hope.
But all I see is the open Road.
What shall I do?

Are you a friend?
Ryan Seemangal

A road with two men, Je m'appelle Ryan, are you a friend? The smell of death lingering in my nose, resembling the firemen using their hose, I see a man not too far; he looks like he

just left the bar. The sight of beer hurting my eyes, the sight of dead flies roaming my lies. I get closer and it hits my nose Jean Paul Gautier le beau le rose. I notice now the man may be dead and in a last ditch attempt is it all in my head.

The mountainous burdens of being 1st place
Emma Dang

Once you are the best, can your skill still lengthen?

No, once you're the best, you peak the very top of the mountain

you stand at its pinnacle, looking down from the summit

It should make you feel prideful, but it's doesn't, far from it

all your life you had strived so hard to be the best.

you had climbed through endless difficulties. And put yourself to the test.

you have pushed away countless opportunities and removed all diversions

And kept your determination close to your chest

But once you are at the top, it gets lonely, with no one to meddle

There can only be one person as the best, 2 players can't have the golden medal

You had succeeded, but at what cost? When you're the best, what could feel better?

The thing is there's no one to triumph with, no one who can share your victory together

Everyone looks up to you below the mountain. there's so much pressure and weight to hold

And alas you carry these burdens alone, as all the others rely on you, the boldest of bold

Desire is the greatest punishment that we bring upon ourselves,

Desires are infinitely boundless, we chase them like predators chasing prey

But unbeknownst to us, we are prey to our desires

And sooner or later, they could consume us one day

Others become envious, others become dependent on you

every single person below only makes the weight stronger

you no longer have a sense of purpose

all you do is stand there, carrying expatriations you want to carry no longer

If you let go of everything you're holding it falls onto everyone else

You don't want that feeling of shame, so you keep holding on

you want to let go of everything though, as it gets more and more unbearable to hold

And although you know it won't, you keep telling yourself the struggle can't keep going on

Was it really worth your time to trek to the top of the mountain? Was it worth the climb?

the only direction you can go in now is down

until you reach the bottom, where you'll find the one thing you never thought you'd find

Defeat. The one thing you've been looking down on, yet now it's something you won't mind

Love
Gurlovoleen Kaur

Love is a song
That everybody craves to sing
Love is a rhythm
That everyone rhymes about

Love is freedom
That everybody wants
Love is like poetry
Only some people could do perfectly

Love is a bird
That everyone wants to fly with
Love is an emotion
That everybody feels everyday

Love is a letter
That everybody craves to receive
Love is an open book
That only some could find the meaning of

Love is Honesty
That only few people give
Love is true
That people can't speak

Love is a bond
That can be made in many relationships
Love is food
That is essential in people's life

Love is a lifetime thing
That this gen-z can't do
Love is soulmate
That is not about betraying people

Love is loyalty
That this generation can't give
Love is life
That some have permanent in their lives

Love is a sign
That only some could understand
Love is being someone's permanent
That is so rare

Never Give Up
Yasemin Mergen

I believe I can beat any challenger but I'm not afraid to lose.
Faith be with the warrior that challenges me,
Because they are in the fight of their lives.
For I will not be a stepping stone to their victory.
They will have to earn their victory over me.

If I lose, I will hold me head up at the end of the challenge,
I will shake the hand of my opponent,
And be respectful and fair with my opponent.

But I will come back and fight for my victory,
And wait for the challenge of another gladiator

To fight his way to the top, where I am waiting;
Waiting, training, and hungry for the next battle.
I will never give up.

A Journey Begins
Julian Woskowiak

In the realm of dreams and endless skies,
A world of wonder, where imagination flies.
Where stars dance in a ballet,
And moonlight shows a magical display
Through the forests, we shall roam,
In search of secrets, yet to be known.
Where whispers of ancient tales unfold
And legends of heroes, brave and bold
With each step, a journey begins,
As we chase the sun and embrace the winds.
Through mountains tall and valleys deep,
Adventures await, secrets to keep.

The Colossal Road
Rida Rizvi

To be alone is not to be lonely.
To venture is not to be clueless.
But one must galvanize others,
In a quest of awakening,
In a quest where one experiences true pleasure.
The pleasure of nature's finest beauties:
the splashes of the serene waterfall,
the beam of the Sun's rays,
its light glistening on the leaf's dew,
the rush of the soft breeze,
the feeling of your bare feet,
standing on something so new,
but something that has always been there.
It calls out to you, "Je suis juste là."

Do not live your life in melancholy.
Do not ask for anymore,
as what you have around you is sufficient.
It is a miracle in itself.
So take advantage,
for that road in front of you,
beckons for your story to be inscribed all over it.
The colossal road does not repudiate,
so do not hesitate.
It promises to alleviate all complications.
It promises the beauties that you will not perceive anywhere else.
So walk along the golden bridge of possibilities,
and cherish what has been and what will be.
For the magnanimous road is there through the storm until daybreak.

True
Henry Sinchi

In the path of hard work, I find my true wealth.

In the maze of life, I find myself in,
In a world where strength really matters.
Every time I try, I show my bright spirit,
Through tough times, I show myself worthy.

I don't give in to sadness or let myself get down,
In tough times, I keep going.
Every time I face a setback, I learn,
In life's tough times, I grow stronger.

The world might doubt me, and fate might laugh,
But I keep pushing forward with determination.
In tough times, I find my happiness,
As I navigate through life's challenges without giving up.

So let the winds blow and the wind to roar,
In the heart of the storm, I won't give up.
I understand life's true meaning with every breath,

In the journey of perseverance, I find my true strength.

Machines of the Open Road
Gavin Dometiza

In the break of dawn, I hear the rumble of power,
Sleek, metal bodies, shining in the morning light,
Speed demons ready to devour the open road,
Their engines purring with a fierce delight.

Each one a masterpiece of engineering art,
Born from the dreams of visionaries bold,
Speeding through the highways, tearing apart,
Miles of asphalt as your stories are told.

From the sleek lines of a Koenigsegg's frame,
To the harshness of a Mustang's growl,
These cars ignite a fiery flame,
In the hearts of those who hear their howl.

They are more than just a piece of steel
They are the embodiment of freedom call
A symphony of engines that you can feel
As they conquer each twist and turn of the track or road's sprawl.

You are the poetry of speed,
A compound of metal and muscle,
Whilst in your seats, we find the thrill we need
To chase our dreams, to hustle and bustle.

And so, let us ride these carriers of joy,
Because they are more than just cars,
They represent freedom's ploy, Giving
our lives something to enjoy.

The Light of the Open Road
Shreya Thomas

Cluelessly, I stumble upon the open road

I know not what lies ahead, nor where I shall go

A small voice calls to me from afar

"Do not be afraid young one, continue forward"

Compelled with the mysterious speaker, I obey, placing one foot in front of the other

Swaying with every blind step, like a dandelion in the wind

A small light glows in the distance, faintly lighting up the dark road

The light brightens my soul, burning inside me with a fiery desire etched into my soul

I must reach the light.

I run through the darkness, with the creatures of the shadows gnashing at my feet.

Their icy grips reach to wrap themselves around my body, slowly consuming my very being.

The alluring scent of the distant flame dies away as I surrender to the dust, melting away like wax on the open road.

Heavy chains hold me down, I stop fighting to break free

My breathing slows as the air begins to feel heavy

"Don't"

The voice slashes through the air like a blade, awakening me from my trance

The stranger stands above me, Her skin glowing, her smile gentle

As she grabs my hand and lifts me up, her touch fills me with life, the chains that bound me loosen their grip

Holding my palms in hers, she whispers kindly "You must go on"

Pulling me by the hand, she leads the way

The path glows with her every step as I see the light from afar shining brighter than before

Together we tread along the path, inching closer to the light

My legs grow weary, giving out beneath me as my eyes marvel at the sight bestowed upon me

Before us stands the light, A small candle, glowing ever so vigilantly

I reach to cup the light in my palms, never wanting the light to fade

A flash blinds me as the world bursts with sudden color and joy

The weeds and thorns retreat into the shadows, only to be replaced by luscious flowers

A soft wind blows as the sky glows with shades of pink and orange

I watch as the flowers wave to the trees, I close my eyes and smile, realizing well that I have reached the light

The open road has led me to the light.

In the forest
Michael Goldthwaite

In the forest, I roam and play,
With animals that come my way.
The trees sway in the gentle breeze,
As the sun shines through the leaves with ease.

I pick wildflowers, colorful and bright,
And watch birds take flight in the light.
The sound of the river flowing by,
Brings a smile to my face as I lie.

I love nature, it's so grand,
With mountains, rivers, and endless land.
I feel at peace when surrounded by trees,
Nature's beauty brings me to my knees.

I'll explore and discover more,
Nature's wonders I'll adore.
In the wilderness, I'll always be,
A part of nature, wild and free.

The rustle of leaves, the whisper of wind,
Nature's lullaby, so sweet and kind.
I climb over rocks and through tall grass,
Every step a new adventure, never to pass.

Birds chirping, bees buzzing,
Nature's symphony, so mesmerizing.
I feel connected to the earth below,
In nature's embrace, my spirit grows.

The warm sun on my face,
As I find my peaceful place.
I breathe in the fresh air so clean,
Nature's magic can truly be seen.

Butterflies flutter by in colors so bright,
I watch them dance in the clear sunlight.
Squirrels scamper up trees so tall,
I admire their agility, never to fall.

In the forest, I feel so alive,
Nature's wonders will forever thrive.
I'll cherish this bond, so pure and true,
In the great outdoors, my heart anew.

Time passing
Halyn Kwon

As I get older, I head towards the road.

The road that leads to my future.

The road, blank with no sense of life around.

I see an empty path that leads to nothing.

What is my future leading to?

Where am I going to go?

Do I follow this mysterious road?

I start my journey on this road.

There is slight greenery filling the emptiness around the road.

The first hurdle appears.

A group of people running towards me.

As they pass by, only negative sayings about me come out of their mouths.

It starts to weaken me, but I push through this road.

It felt like eternity while they ran past me.

As I trudge along the road, I come across some flowers and trees planted by the side of the road.

As the aroma of the flowers spread, it gave me hope.

It gave me a feeling of comfort.

Would I be able to make it through this road?

With a sudden aspiration I am able to make it through the road.

Soon I pass several hurdles.

It seems that it will never end.

Will I have to do this for the rest of my life?

Every hurdle I go through is either a hardship or an accomplishment.

Some good and some bad.

I soon realize that this is how life goes.

Our lives aren't perfect and we will have our ups and downs.

Things will push us down while other things may push us up.

It is all a part of life and with the right people and the right mindset, we can push through.

It may take a while but that's what's part of the journey.

Everybody has their own road and their own paths.

Fork Road
Anusha Shah

In front of me, like everyone, there lies a path
A path to the future but it all seems bad
One fork leads to an end that I find quite sad
The other however, seems like a fad
I look back to the first fork and wonder if I should follow the rest
But before I choose I take a breath,
Looking back at the road time is running out
I flip a coin but catch it before it hits the ground
I don't need chance to tell me what to choose
I walk in between the route to watch the view
Looking from both sides the grass looks vert
But there is still no fate that is calling to me
Here in the middle the plants grow most
Rose, jaune, bleu, they're all a host
For bees and pollen the world is buzzing with hope
And with not a soul around me, I have looked
This path was the best choice because it was mine
And I will follow it through, maybe, for the rest of time.

A Heart for a Brain
Melissa Lee

Down that Summer Road I held my tears
No more backing down time to face my fears
This road would lead to love or a broken heart
Well my journey begins, but Do I want to start?

With every doubtful stride my foot sunk down
"Don't go on Melissa it's time to turn around"
Mrs, Moon frowned upon me as I stopped in place
Mr. Wind pushed me back into this internal race

On with my quest to tell this boy how I feel
A love I've never felt, this must be real
The road seemed to darken as I neared his house
I can do this, I can do this, I'm not a scared little mouse

Hope took me by my hand and knocked on the door
Fear grabbed me by the neck and struck my aching core
I've lost all control of my heartbeat now
Got caught on this open road with him somehow

The door creaked open as his figure stood tall
I gulped and I shivered, feeling stupid and small
"I have something to tell you, don't tell a soul"
"But i think I like you," my heart did a roll

A look on his face, an expression so odd
The only words that escaped his lips? "Oh god."

Basketball
Divjot Nayyar

I write about hoops and the embrace of the court,
where athletes hustle and don't waste time.
The action takes place on a hardwood stage.
A series of steps performed while telling stories.

Basketball is a hard-core sport where skill fits talent.
From the baseline to the exquisiteness of the rim,
A battlefield where abilities endure,
40 minutes a game where talents are displayed.

The sound of sneakers squeaking,
players grinding, no turning around.
They dribble, shoot, and glide ferociously here in this stadium,
full of pride and perspiration.

The ball, a soaring celestial like a meteor,
Silent joy through hoops and nets.
The scoreboard roars, and there are cheers.
In this intensely tense game.

Rebounds in a tight jam
as the clock ran out in the hard grind of paint.
Three-pointers and the embracing of arc
A court that moves at an unrelenting speed.

The unadorned performance in the world of basketball,
where only the best will prosper,
A woven tapestry of victories,
the spirit of the game, in the sunlight.

Transition
Kapish Pharma

In the halls full of people, where dreams may start,
Where minds bloom, like plants in the ground.
The transition from the kid's world to the adult's,
I am on the road of high school.

Names called in the air, pencils scratching, Through
classes where echoes of learning resound, There is
noise I yearn for the most.
RIIIIIIIING, the final bell tolls.

The chemicals from the lab wafting through my nose,
The chocolate milk I struggle to swallow,
The pressure from my peers,
I am stuck in a cycle of despair.

But along this high school road I tread
I realize the mistakes I've made.
Instead of looking at school with dread,
There is always the chance to seize the day.

There may be twists and turns with every stride,
But I have my comrades by my side.
My friends, my allies, my support, Fighting
through the trials and tribulations.

The flame from which student's candles burn bright,
The masters of knowledge,
Those who aid students on their paths,
I call them my teachers.

Growth and opportunity lurk behind every corner,
But I only see stress and work.
As I travel down the road of high school,
There must be change.

But maybe from me...

Made to Defy
Jasmine Sharma

Not a dime in my pocket left to spare,
I wrote this poem for the world to share,
I was made to cook, to clean, to satisfy
But sometimes I couldn't help but cry.
In a world where women were expected to comply,
I don't know why but I was tempted to defy,
I wish to soar across the sky,
I wish everyday was like an open road waiting as my guide
Today I don't know what might happen,
But I do know I'll show my voice to all those higher ups with poise.
I know I may sound somewhat foolish but isn't this my life to live,
How much longer must we comply,
How much longer must we perform as puppets,
The world will once know the pain and power held by a women,
We weren't just made to cook and clean and satisfy,
We were made to defy.

Correspondances
Dalia Rguigue

Oui, a journey, a new journey.
Où irons nous?
Perhaps la plage ou les montagnes?
Maybe a familiar place I've been to?
I remember a place with un champ ouvert.
L'air pur et calme,no worries to be found.
L'herbe très verte et filled with many creatures.
Insectes et animaux of all kinds.
The sounds of the birds fill my ears. C'est beau et gentil.
Pendant que je marche, je vois des fleurs.
I pick one up, and take a sniff.
Sweet nectar scent.
Pollen stains my fingers, as I take a glimpse of a papillon.
It soon flies away as I try to get closer.
I move on,then I'm faced with an issue.
Which path shall I take, gauche ou droite.
Alors, je vois un groupe d'amis.
I think I'm lost, I say, and they guide me to another world.
Un beau village, filled with smiles.
They show me around and learn that the most simple things are the prettiest.
L'odeur de la boulangerie, the sound of laughter, the touch of the earth, overwhelms me.
They have given me the taste of nature.
But, I had to go, all journeys come to an end.

Home
Kayla Birch

The seashore, it provided comfort
The soft sand brought many memories
The bright blue sea in the distance, allowing
freedom and tranquility
The laughter from the people
that echoed through my ears
It was not only refreshing but fulfilling
The air of which I breathed
cool and a gift
The sun of which rays had warmth and security
Shined down on me
This was home, this was safe
I have learned happiness, friendship, peace
I've learned it all here
The beach parties, the bonfires
The talks, advice, tears, laughs and games
Where we all connected as one.
Sometimes disagreements tore us apart
but in the end this beach brought us back together
This was our safe place
Where we met and where we departed
Now I stand alone on this seashore
Watching others connect just as we did
This was my road. My home.

Delusions and Dreams
Neel Tripathi

Je woke up, looked out the window,
It was snowing that morning,
And I got ready to prepare for mon voyage.

I descended down the stairs,
I ate food,
And I prepared for mon voyage.

I brushed my teeth,
I put on socks,
I put on my joote (shoes),
And I left for mon voyage.

I opened the car door,
Step in,
Sat down,
And we set off for mon voyage.

Mon voyage,
What is it?
Mon voyage is my basketball tournament,
To decide if I make the team or not.

I get out the gade (car),
Grab my topi (hat),
And my ball,
And get to the court.

Me and my mon amis,
We stretch,
Hop on the court,
And prepare to play.

Fast forward to the end of the game.

The score is 20-20,
To win we need 21,
The other team just missed,
We have the ball.

My friend dribbles down the court,
And he passes to me,
I shoot it,
I miss it.

The other team gets the ball,
They dribble down the court,
The guy gets ready to shoot,
He is defended by 3 people,
He shoots,
He makes it.

I woke up.
It was all a dream,
A delusion.

Dreams,
Very real and also not,
like mon voyage.

Delusions,
even though this was going to happen anyways,
My brain still fooled me, it tricked me into thinking it was really happening.
I only chose to call this a delusion because,
Like Mike Tyson said,
Delusions are only delusions when those delusions haven't become a reality,
Like mon voyage.

The Future in My Hands
Sara Bakhteri

Facing the life I left behind,
Losing hope of its return.
Quickly, I push my past out of my mind,
With hesitation and a sudden head turn.
I feign excitement and face the division of paths ahead of me.

North, East, and West, each road tempting one thing
North, I see a loving family, with a lack of wealth
East, all the riches in the world, wasted on a life with no meaning
In the West, surrounded by everything I've dreamt of while suffering from poor health
Love, Money, Success, each one accompanied by a sacrifice.

Standing face-to-face with my fate,

I absorb the serene environment one last time

Taking in the fresh air and distinct smell of flowers I've come to appreciate
A final swim in the lake and sunset by the shoreline.
Coming to terms with the end of my childhood and the start of the future.

With a deep breath, I advance straight ahead North

After all, a life filled with love is the richest life one could live
Putting more force on the gas pedal, I leave my past behind.
Eagerly, I face adulthood with my intuition to guide me.

Home
Sumer Hussaini

The sound of my foot against the gravel fills my ears
The open road welcomes me
Behind me, I leave all my fears
I step towards what i cannot see

The road ahead is unknown
What will I find at the end?
I continue walking, alone
A second chance is waiting at the bend

Hope pulls me onwards
This escape is my only solution
The light I walk towards,
Fills me with determination

My past is far behind me
Aimlessly I roam
I am met with a sense of safety
At last I am home

To Adorn
Harmanpreet Kaur

A big, long road
Silent and calm.
The chirps of birds
With one lone voice,
The voice of my breath.
No one but me
And some majestic trees.
I look beneath me,
And there lies my name.
This path belongs to me
It carries hardships and cherished memories
Building strength, knowing me down
It whispers sweetly, scolds harshly,
However, it is my path alone,
My journey to Adorn.

The Long Road
Fouzia Khan

The road is long
sometimes I take the way that's wrong
I wonder when I'll get there
But then ask myself what is taking so long
I look around It's an empty road
I pray and I pray that I get there safe
Hoping there is a way out of this empty place
After a while I find a sign that leads me to the right way
There is a smile on my face
I am almost at my location but Its dark
I came out when It was bright
I wonder what took me long
But then remember I took the wrong way.

On the open road
Aareez Umar Siddiqui

1

On the open road, carefree and light,
No more whining, just joy which feels so right.
The path ahead, wherever I choose,
No need for luck, my destiny I conduct

2

Learning lessons of acceptance, also reflectance
From wild to wise, no need for perfection.
Shapes and colors speak, like a boutique
Walking on paths worn, ready to learn.

3

The earth is my canvas, so I'm not anxious
Breaking free from my limits, no need to count my minutes
Breathing in space, the east, the west, all mine.

4

Encounters with a thousand of faces, so grand,
In the open air, nous pouvons tout faire
Happiness surrounds, which we have all found
In this endless race, we all have our own pace

5

Sailing on the endless seas, with an open breeze
Obstacles ahead, no time for bed
But the road calls, an adventure dawns

6
Journeying with friends, seeing through a different lens
Endless roads merging into cool journeys,
A universe of senses, no need for expenses

7
Through teenage struggles, a goal in demand,
Active rebellion, courage firsthand.
Armed with dreams, facing teenage strife,
Helpers by my side, making the journey rife.

8
The road is before me, tested and safe,
Unwritten papers, unopened books, ready to chafe.
Leave tools behind, let money remain unearned,
Knowledge will be my goal.

Creating a Road
Sahil Qureshi

A road, if only it were as simple as that.

Told to show others the road I'm on.

I'm looking behind me as I try to think about the story I've lived.

The farther I look back, the more weak and cracked it seems.

It is a road, though it's one that had to go through many stories to become a road.

It has cracks inconsistently throughout the path.

Some carried footsteps that were heavier than others.

Some carried what felt like boulders that could've made the entire road collapse.

But it's still a road that worked just right for me.

And now that I look ahead, I see nothing.

The path is empty.

There is no road ahead.

And that excites me.

I get to pave the road now.

It is my turn to create the stories that created the road I stand on.

Where will I go?

What will I see?

These are questions I'll answer while creating this road.

I will find the answers to where I'll go.

I'll meet who will help me create this road.

I'll see places that inspire me to keep building this road.

I'll see what makes building this road worth it.

I wish this were easy, though.

I wish that my hands wouldn't get tired.

I wish that my legs wouldn't grow older the more I build.

It gets harder every day I spend making this road.

But the road and I get stronger too.

And by the end of this, it'll be a road made of diamond.

And my hands will be able to carry the boulders that made it so difficult building it.

Roam
Daiwik Uppal

In the vast glorified space of time,
Where freedom breaks with chains of restraints,
Amidst the echoes of souls long gone,
We journey forth, never-ending.

The route before us, unoccupied, unretained,
With struggles and wars, we are not constrained.
For every success, a repercussion awaits,
A longing for battle, a destiny that subsides grace.

In the depths of darkness, we find no light,
Helplessly searching, we take all night.
Our existence, a fleeting moment in the grand design,
Yet in this insignificance, there can be seen something bright..

We wander, seeking truth,
Exploring until we aren't.
No historical figures can meet our endeavors,
With what's to come meeting the land's horizon.

Let us roam, Let me roam.
Until I surrender, I fear no
danger.

Though people live misery, born with or without, In the court of existence, we provide the way out. A journey of solitude, commitment, choice,
In the depths of our souls, we unearthed a strong compelling voice.

Ignore the voice at hand, journey apart, Leave man behind, left in the dark.
For in the end, it's not about how we go, But the way in which we all choose to do so.

Honorable Mentions

Vastness
Melissa Martin – Period 1

EASTPORT-SOUTH MANOR JR./SR. HIGH SCHOOL

Kosta Calandra
Max Ferraro
Thomas Lally
Jake Misciagno
Lizbeth Sebastian Francisco
Jaden Ceredo-Hidalgo
Jeremy Goeta
Kelly Loja Jarama
Victor Soler
Nolan Douglas
Xavier Harris
Gavin Mazovec
Emmanuel Skepple

Paths Unpaved
Shannon Murphy – Grade 9, Period 3

OYSTER BAY HIGH SCHOOL

Genesis Alvarez-Hernandez
Mia Carleo
Savanna Gallo
Aari Gupta
Alisa Kelly
Benjamin Lingen
Vladimir Morales
Isabella Rizzuto
Chiara Sherwood
Thomas Vidro
Nina Ballone
Carew Davis
Nicole Gatti
Kaya Harrison
Elise Kim
Chae Lordi
William Nobel
Chloe Romano
Sophia Staphos
Emme Carleo
Caitlin Dias
Chloe Gheerow
Jake Kansler
Luke Kugler
Payton Miraglia
Sophia Pavlovic
Craig Shelley
Chrysta Thomas

Avenues Await
Shannon Murphy – Grade 9, Period 9

OYSTER BAY HIGH SCHOOL

Samuel Brenner
Christos Kokotos
Kaela Miley
Brandon Sattar
AnaLuz Ferrer
Maalika Mehta
Owen J. Mitchell
Danny Yanes Mejia
Emma Hampton
Mikal Memon
Clare Murcott
Delmy Zavala Chicas

CLASS ANTHOLOGY, GRADES 11 & 12

Category K

Grand Champion

The Road of Desire
Dr. Deirdre Faughey—Grade 11, Period 2

OYSTER BAY HIGH SCHOOL

Dance and Soul
Sophia Guerrero

In the heart of the city that never sleeps,
Where dreams are born and music seeps,
New York, a symphony of rhythm and rhyme,
Where melodies dance and souls intertwine.

High Heels click on the city street,
As music's beat guides fashionable feet.
Designer dresses and tailored suits,
Fashion and music, a harmonious pursuit.

From hop-hop to punk, and everything in between,
New York's music scene is a vibrant scene.
It unites us all, from every walk of life,
Bringing joy, healing wounds, and soothing Strife.

Let the music guide you through the city's beat,
Feel the rhythm, embrace the heat.
New York City, a melody so grand,
A place where music and dreams expand.

Bright White Coat
Jane Gurney

The road is rocky, so I see
But that never scared me
I know that it will take a lot of time
But I won't stop until what I want is mine
I will meet people who will help and care
Which in this world is often rare
I see the light at the end of the tunnel
But I know to get there will take hustle
I know I want that bright white coat
And so I will take note
On those who have succeeded
Who have helped those that needed
I know that it will take a while
So I won't act juvenile
I will control what I can
To finish out my plan
I can see it clearly now
Me, taking a bow
In that bright white coat

What I'm Doing Here
Jackson Kelly

Still young and stupid I look down upon a tattered and bendy road,
With hills stretching high and low as far as the eye can see
Along this road
People will tell you that
Simplicity leads to happiness,
But life's viscosity is seemingly preventing so
Our minds,
Wired to simple dopamine loops yearn for the deeper complexities of our own lives,
And yet
We always find what we don't like the most
We know life has something deeper
Some of us seemingly already found simplicity,
Outside the loop
Some of us feel it sometimes,
But it's never really there
And still
I always find what I don't like the most
I know there's more to uncover in the catacombs of time
Trust the process
Settle down and take it easy
I'm still young
And it's my own fault
Or whatever they say

I Know the Narrow Road
Adrian Kim

I know
the road paved with clay bricks,
where the sun admits its glorious favor,
and the feathered notes of wings form a sweet melody.

Yet I know
the earth's disguise of shadows,
and at the end of it all,
is a silent void, where echoes of somber absence resonate.

I know
where the path diverges into a narrow road,
where the sun whispers its subdued glow,
and the midnight's echo of a raven's crow weaves shadows into the clouds.
Fallen trees and barriers arise,
as the eager spirit gradually dies,
while delay fails time, and withdrawal strips life.

Yet I know
that the moon and stars bear witness,
and hearten the weary soul,
and at the end of it all,
is a sanctuary of tranquility and wonder,
free from the chains of deception.
A place of beautiful reward.

On the Road Again
Alexa Laurencon

I'm on the road again.
Vibrant green trees lead me on a continuous trail of hope.
Sun radiates on my windshield, mirroring my smile.
I'm surrounded by everything
but I'm alone.

I'm on the road again.
The fresh air enters my body as stress exits
a new start to my life.
Endless chances of freedom and possibilities
are beyond the horizon.

I'm on the road again.
Birds chirp as they glide beyond my sight.
Trees wave with the wind as I pass.
Tires meet the concrete
as they embark on their new journey.

I'm on the road again.
A new adventure emerges
as I reach my destination.
I become stationary again,
pondering about my adventure.

I can't wait to get on the road again.

The Voices
Rose Lindstrom

The walls of the museum echo with the voices of the past,
And although you think you can only hear the creaky floorboards
    underneath your feet,
Centuries of people,
Great people,
Horrible people,
Interesting people,
Ignored people,
Are talking to you.
Through the delicate hands that stroked the paintbrush for the art on the
    wall,
To the rough hands that built the floorboards you're standing on,
Everyone has a story to tell.
Time doesn't exist in this dimension,
And I could listen to the people all day.
In one day I could dive into humanity's worst sufferings,
And feel the pain and regret of the past,
Or I could discover society's greatest gifts,
And feel happiness filling my stomach.
By the time the announcement of the museum's closing rings through the
    halls,
I'm unaware of how I ended up here in the first place,
And as my feet guide me to the exit,
I look back to the road I took within this museum,
To visit everyone,
And hear their voices,
Because one day,
I will too,
Become a voice of history.

The Road to Success
Michael Olivero

The road I take is one which has been traveled many times.
It's a path worn deep from those who have followed it through the ages.
The route to success has been clearly laid on this path.
Many travel along this road,
the narrow, mud spattered path stays jammed with people trying to march forward.
As I trek along this path,
I sit and observe.
Many have been taken by the road.
People hurt people,
purposely pushing other towards the flames of corruption,
or the poison of addiction
for the selfish purpose of getting ahead in the pack.
I watch as the person burned slowly loses themselves behind others marching forward
not even glancing at the man being trampled on the beat down path.
I see the bitterness in the man's eyes as he lays on the floor, defeated
as he slowly picks himself up,
he brings others down in order to get back to where he was.
With this,
the cycle of hurt continues on the path
multiplying like a virus,
the hate spewed bitterness takes over the path until chaos erupts
now no one can go forward on the path
apart from those already in front of the violence.

Looking Past the Fog
Anastasia Sakellis

One foot forward I approach diverging paths
standing at the crossroads unaware.
Clouds loom overhead casting shadows of uncertainty
with one foot forward I approach blindly.

The road may twist and turn, obscured from sight
even so I follow my feet,
step by step,
venturing down the road as the breeze follows me.

Looking past the fog ahead, I listen.
I listen to the breeze.
I listen to the whispers.
I am not alone on my path.

Others surround me.
My path is not my own.
They too have to look past the fog
and find their way.

The Walk into Town
Jack Sapienza

As I travel down the old open road
with only the dimly light street lights
and the old gravel path on the side
I hear the gravel crunching under my feet.

As I travel into town
I travel past the old stores and restaurants
with the slight hum of the neon lights
and the wind of the cars passing by me.

As I get closer to the town,
the gravel becomes pavement
and the street lights up.

What once were the ancient run-down stores
become newer and more popular.
The old becomes the new
the closer you get into town.

The Open Road of Desire
Connor Walsh

The open road of desire
I embark on the open road of desire.
On this road there is a finish line in sight,
however many roadblocks along the way.
Each time the road gets closer to the finish line
the self-consciousness extends the finish line farther away.
The finish line looks to be as bright as the stars,
the closer the stars get, the brighter they are.
But the stars never get closer, because of self interference.
The road of desire, is one that is rewarding
but the self imposed speed bumps along the way, make it torturing.

This road includes a lot of people:
the ones who give support
and the ones who try to tear you farther from the destination.
Ignore the doubts and the road to desire
could spark a fire in your heart, to do something you admire.

Honorable Mentions

The Next Road
Deidre Faughey, Grade 11, Period 4

OYSTER BAY HIGH SCHOOL

Jenna Angelidakis
Gwenyth Davey
Omar Figueroa
Ella Reardon-Rizzo
Scarlett Shelley

Brandon Antonetti
Grace Egan
Emily Murphy
Amelia Scamell

Road Conditions
Dr. Maria Kim – Grade 11 period 1

OYSTER BAY HIGH SCHOOL

Austin Aschettino
Mihail Dajko
Olivia Garcia
Joe Laurita
James Salvato

Landon Baugh
Holly Emerson
Max Lapidus
Jane Myers

Sunshowers
Dr. Maria Kim – Grade 11 period 8

OYSTER BAY HIGH SCHOOL

Taha Gulkaya
Dylan Kieran
Khadeejah Memon
Samantha Myers
Graciela Romero
Audrey Underberg

Tyler Kamback
Cristiana Martorella
Hayden Mentzinger
Lauren Pinnock
Angel Sarabia
John Musso

Multimedia

Category L

Grand Champion

A Journey into the Unknown
Madison Kelly

In life's journey, a winding road awaits me,
Filled with twists and turns and ups and downs.
The road ahead of me is still uncertain,
So I don't know what lies ahead of me.

I search for a map, a sign
To cast light upon the darkness of the unpredictability of my future,
And the answer to where my road in life will lead,
Only to hope that one day the answer will be revealed.

My future right now is like a canvas,
And it's a blank blur filled with emptiness.
My canvas is not yet painted, but with every step of the way, it begins to paint itself.
What will be waiting for me at the end of my road?

Will I be successful and achieve my goals, or stumble and fail?
Will I have to climb over steep mountains or walk across tiny hills?
Will I have to sail across stormy seas or be met with calm waves?
Will harsh lightning strike, or will gentle raindrops fall from the sky?

No matter what happens, I'll never shelter myself from the storm.
I'll always dance in the rain.
I won't be afraid of what is to come,
Because with every twist and turn comes a lesson learned.

The pieces of my puzzle will come together,
Replacing my blank canvas with vivid colors bold and bright.
My dreams spread across my canvas,
Painting a beautiful, vibrant sunset to guide me on my journey.

I'll trust myself to face the unknown with a smile,
Because that's part of what makes life so exciting.
I'll follow my heart and reach for the stars
As I sit back and watch my story unfold.

Category L, Multimedia 177
MOUNT SINAI MIDDLE SCHOOL
Mrs. Wallace

www.ingramcontent.com/pod-product-compliance
Lightning Source LLC
Chambersburg PA
CBHW061735070526
44585CB00024B/2685